Alina Polyak

The Role of Religion - Tradition and Modernity in Contemporary Jewish American Literature

GRIN Verlag

Bibliografische Information der Deutschen Nationalbibliothek:

Die Deutsche Bibliothek verzeichnet diese Publikation in der Deutschen National-
bibliografie; detaillierte bibliografische Daten sind im Internet über http://dnb.d-
nb.de/ abrufbar.

Imprint:

Copyright © 2009 GRIN Verlag GmbH
Druck und Bindung: Books on Demand GmbH, Norderstedt Germany
ISBN: 978-3-640-38433-4

This book at GRIN:

http://www.grin.com/en/e-book/132426/the-role-of-religion-tradition-and-moder-
nity-in-contemporary-jewish-american

GRIN - Your knowledge has value

Der GRIN Verlag publiziert seit 1998 wissenschaftliche Arbeiten von Studenten, Hochschullehrern und anderen Akademikern als eBook und gedrucktes Buch. Die Verlagswebsite www.grin.com ist die ideale Plattform zur Veröffentlichung von Hausarbeiten, Abschlussarbeiten, wissenschaftlichen Aufsätzen, Dissertationen und Fachbüchern.

Visit us on the internet:

http://www.grin.com/

http://www.facebook.com/grincom

http://www.twitter.com/grin_com

Abschlussarbeit

zur Erlangung des Magister Artium im Fachbereich Amerikanistik

der Johann Wolfgang Goethe-Universität

Institut für England- und Amerikastudien

"The Role of Religion: Tradition and Modernity in

Contemporary Jewish American Literature."

vorgelegt von: Alina Polyak

aus: Kiew

Einreichungsdatum: 24.03.2009

Table of contents.

1. Introduction   **3**

1.1 Historical overview   8

1.2 Christianity as a "default" religion   9

1.3 Conversion to Judaism   11

1.4 Substitutes for religion   15

1.5 Antisemitism   17

2. Religious sources   **21**

2.1 Folklore and mysticism: Golem and reincarnation   26

3. Place   **36**

3.1 The Lower East Side   37

3.2. Israel   40

3. 3. Europe   52
    3.3.1 Ukraine   53
    3.3.2 Germany   56

4. Language   **62**

4.1 Hebrew   63

4.2 Yiddish   65

4.3 English   70

4.4 Name and Identity   72

5. Jewish tradition and feminism in women's writing   **77**

6. Food and ritual   **87**

7. Conclusion   **99**

8. Works cited: **105**

9. Abstract (Zusammenfassung)   **110**

1. Introduction

The search for the roots has become a major issue in contemporary American society. The tendency to seek one's origins finds its reflection in many aspects of popular culture including art and literature. It seems that American society is witnessing a revival of ethnic roots and has been lately passing from a "melting pot" to a "boiling cauldron" of multicultural, multiethnic and multilingual America, where people of different origins coexist.

The recently coined term "hyphenated Americans" reflects the tendency of Americans looking for ethnic identity. It shows that one's identity can be multiple and one side of the hyphen does not necessarily have to exclude the other. Different cultures are influenced by American mainstream culture, and mainstream culture is in turn influenced by different traditions. In the final analysis, the mainstream culture becomes enriched through all the different influences. There are no restrictions about who writes about what. White authors can write about black characters, Chinese authors about Jewish characters, male authors about female characters etc. The centrality of Christian tradition remains rooted in American culture and literature, but with the new trend of ethnic multicultural writing, other traditions and rituals are represented to the general audience as well. These ethnic writers who are "insiders" in their culture often criticize traditional practices, which are largely unknown to the general public. This is also true for the Jewish American writing.

Hana Wirth-Nesher points out that although Jewish American writing shares many features with other ethnic literature in the United States, its singularity is that it also entails a religious dimension. The Jewish identity is redefined as a faith rather than as civilization and the separation of church and state in the United States has transformed Jews into adherents of Judaism ("Traces of the Past," 119). It seems that by the end of the twentieth century, the approach to religion and to identity, which in case of Judaism overlap, has taken a new turn. Many novels are being written by writers knowledgeable in Jewish tradition and lore, using Jewish languages, figures of Jewish folklore and religious notions. Jewishness is not something to be ashamed of anymore.

It is not an easy task to define what Jewish American literature is, whether this definition depends on author's religious faith, ethnicity, range of themes, languages that the author uses, the use of liturgical texts, etc. Today, the Jewish American writers write in English, their native language, a language of Christian culture, which adapts to the Jewish view of the world, changing and absorbing ideas and words from Hebrew and Yiddish. They write for the mainstream American audience, the majority of which are non-Jewish readers, using notions and ideas which are rooted in the Jewish culture and religion, without explaining or translating them, assuming that their audience is able to understand them without translation.

Ezra Cappell claims that today's writing is the "new American Talmud." The Talmud consists of two distinct parts, the bigger one, which deals with legal issues, the smaller one, the *aggadic* part consisting of stories, homilies, interpretations of biblical passages and advice on ethics.

Cappell compares the *aggadic* section of the Babylonian Talmud in its storytelling aspects with the cultural work of American Jewish fiction.

"...through its literary passages the Talmud reinterprets the Torah anew for its own generation. This open-endedness, this celebration of multiple perspectives, is not only a characteristic of the Babylonian Talmud; it is also a hallmark of twentieth-century and contemporary American Jewish fiction" (2).

According to Cappell, the literary production of Jews in America can be seen as a new layer or a stage of development of rabbinical commentary on the scriptural inheritance of the Jewish people. The center of rabbinic storytelling is scripture and the Jewish American writers also often refer to scripture, sometimes without full awareness of doing so. However they may stray from the Jewish tradition, they often return to the centering force of Judaism: the Scripture and the Holy Books. A book has a deep meaning in symbology in Jewish culture, the Jews are called "the People of the Book." There is a deep respect for knowledge and a book is a storage of knowledge and values. A book that is written by Jewish-Americans metamorphoses into a kind of a metaphysical place for them to explore the impact of identity, be it religious or ethnic.

The defining feature of rabbinic literature is its ongoing interpretation of history. Literature becomes the faith for secular contemporary Jews, a tool to understand and interpret history for future generations. The Jewish American writers have become the theologians of the contemporary Jewish American culture (Cappell, 2-5). Another parallel between the Talmud and modern fiction is the concern for humanity, for moral design and purpose.

Nancy Haggard-Gilson writes that, at least since the 1950's among the second generation American Jews, Judaism has been replaced by "Jewishness." a secular, ethnic culture. The drive for assimilation carried away the religious components replacing them with folk symbols, ethnic food and identification with the State of Israel. She argues that Jewish fiction mirrored the concern with ethnic identity and the flight from Judaism as a response to the pressure to assimilate. But the distinction between "Jewishness" and "Judaism" might be too simplistic. The level of Jewish religious observance is not a defining part of a Jewish identity anymore. Jewish identity can be both religious and cultural, in America it also has a strong ethnic component But the history of Jews does not imply that a lessening of religious practice severs identification with the ideas, ethics and the world views of Judaism. The pursuit of justice and morality, the observing of ethical rules and the identification with the historical experience of the Jewish people, are some of the things which are no less important to Judaism than belief in God, or literacy in Hebrew and Talmud.

Adam Meyer points out that the idea of a return to a religious sense of Judaism came to the forefront in many works of the third generation authors. Instead of "writers who are Jews" they have become "Jewish writers." They have rediscovered their Judaism and retrieved Jewish forms and topics. Meyer quotes Nessa Rappoport's phrase: "Having won our place in American culture, we are beginning to be confident enough to reclaim Jewish culture" (111).
Returning to Jewish values seems to be a major trend and the main feature which makes them different from the previous generations.
There are many thematic fields which are connected to the Jewish identity, whether it is cultural or religious, such as settings in Israel or Jewish Diaspora, issues relevant for Jewish people, use of religious symbols, Hebrew and Yiddish languages. The Jewish identity is inseparable from the Jewish culture, which is in turn inseparable from religion. Judaism is a religion connected to time and memory. In order to consider themselves one religious entity, Jews "must rely upon the recognition of a shared past and tradition to retain continuity and

cohesiveness" (Haggard-Gilson, 24). When writing about Jewish themes which are at a first glance, secular, authors connect to religion through different channels.

L. Stahlberg notes that history or remembrance of history serves God in Judaism. Forgetting history is equated with sinfulness. She suggests that contemporary Jewish literature should be read in light of the past which it reflects. The need to remember is essential in Judaism. Remembering the covenant is as important as keeping it. "Remembering becomes bound up in narrative, in writing and retelling history; keeping is accomplished through ritual observance... Religiously, the focus of memory in Judaism has been on remembering and keeping the commandments, on ritually reenacting the past" (Stahlberg, 74 -75).

The future of Judaism is bound up in remembrance of the past, since the tradition for Jews is a chain that connects past and future generations.

Many of the Jewish rituals, words in Jewish languages, rabbinical commentaries, Torah sources, liturgy fragments etc. are mentioned in contemporary texts without their meanings being explained.

Hana Wirth-Nesher points out that the Jewish American literature has always aimed at a double audience, at the general and the Jewish reader ("Accented Imagination," 290). Although the general American non-Jewish reader might be familiar with some practices of Judaism through popular culture, movies, etc. nevertheless most of the American readers do not have a profound knowledge of the Jewish tradition. Thus, the texts can be understood on different levels. The readers are divided into groups – a smaller group of those who have the knowledge of Judaism, the "in-group readers," and those who have no "insider" knowledge: the "outside" readers.

Early immigrant writers were trying to enter the mainstream literary culture – which they apparently succeeded to do. They had to explain many terms of their culture, which were unknown to the general American audience. Although their native language was in the most cases Yiddish, they nevertheless chose to write in English, their adopted language. English was the means to reach their intended "outsider" audience. For example, they made appendixes of words unfamiliar to their intended non-Jewish American audience, or tried to give intercultural translations. For example, Mary Antin has a glossary which has a key to pronunciation and bracket transcriptions of Hebrew and Yiddish words. Religious rituals and holidays are explained on a basic level. The in-group Jewish reader

does not need these explanations. Werner Sollors mentions in his introduction to Mary Antin's novel that Antin imagines a more hostile Gentile outside reader. She adjusts herself, trying to make her text more understandable: " ...strategy of sometimes addressing, but almost always implying a reader from the outside world have to have certain effects on the writing of such a text: the in-group reader would feel more excluded, and the role of the author as mediator would be strengthened" (Sollors, Introduction, XXI).

Sometimes these explanations were apologetic, building on how the "barbaric" rituals were connected to harsh life conditions in their countries of origin. The immigrant Jewish American novels by Abraham Cahan, Mary Antin and Anzia Yezierska treated the Jewish tradition as a vestige of the Old World, something a Jewish immigrant had to get rid of in order to be accepted in the new society. Today there are hardly any translations or explanations to be found, making higher demands of the reader.

Judith Oster mentions the observations of a sociologist Marcus Lee Hansen who noted the phenomenon of third-generation Americans who are discovering the traditions of their grandparents. What the second-generation wanted to forget, these grandchildren now want to remember. She thinks that there is a literary pattern operating, when the grandchildren are discovering the stories of the grandparents, which were forgotten and discharged. In order to find them again, they go through such hardships as learning their grandparents' languages, be it Yiddish or Chinese. Oster quotes Lan Samantha Chang who coins the term "unforgetting." "Different from merely remembering, unforgetting is the unraveling of the deliberate effort of forgetting" (Oster, 153-154).

In this thesis, I concentrate on Jewish American literature and explore how the search for roots – in this case the roots which are connected to Judaism – is reflected in many novels which are written by American Jewish authors of different generations. I illustrate by examples from contemporary American Jewish writing, comparing the attitudes to Judaism in contemporary and first-generation immigrant writing. I argue that one cannot separate the Jewish ethnic identity, which is a focus of Jewish American literature, from the Jewish religion. Judaism encompasses all aspects of culture and even the most secular of writers relate to Judaism the moment they write about Jewish themes. Even when they choose to assimilate and remove themselves from religion, they would be writing about the religion they have distanced themselves from. In the Jewish context and history, it is impossible to separate the religion from tradition and culture. I explore how different aspects of identity interconnect through religion and how the legacy of the Jewish tradition is reclaimed and reaffirmed by modern authors writing in English. The thematic fields I explore encompass different spheres of life, which are connected to Judaism. The way writers deal with these themes shows the importance (or unimportance) that the religious tradition has for them. Even when they criticize religious ideas, these are Jewish ideas they deal with.

Judaism is something they either reject or embrace, but it is there in their works and it is what makes their writing Jewish American writing.

I would also like to compare the attitude towards religion in the works of first-generation immigrant authors, whose native language was not English, and how this attitude changed with the new generation of writers at the end of the twentieth century.

In order to understand the complexity of the Jewish identity, one needs to know how Jews came to become Americans and to perceive the "golden land" of America (as the common Yiddish phrase went) as the new promised land. America was the final destination for many immigrants and they embraced its values and culture sometimes sacrificing their own cultural values.

1.1 Historical overview

The first Jews ever to set foot on American soil were twenty three refugees from the Dutch colony of Recife in northeastern Brazil in year 1654. Their families had to flee Spain and Portugal when Isabella of Spain ordered all Jews to leave in 1492.

The Jewish immigrants came from Germany and central Europe in 1880's in thousands, but the biggest wave of immigrants came from Eastern Europe

and Russia, fleeing the pogroms between 1880 and 1924. These Jews were
strictly religious and their primary language was Yiddish.

By 1925, there were 4.5 million Jews in the United States, constituting one
of the world's largest communities (Diner, New Promised Land,1-45).

The first Jewish writers who entered the American mainstream belonged to this
wave of immigration. Their native language was Yiddish. For example,
Abraham Cahan wrote both in Yiddish and in English. Their works became a
kind of a bridge between two cultures. Their novels were intended for a Gentile
American Christian reader who did not know much about the Jewish culture.
Mary Antin is trying to describe her becoming an American in terms
understandable for non-Jewish American readers, thus making her immigrant
experience universal. "The making of American" and getting rid of the "old"
identity is a common theme in early immigrant novels.

1.2 Christianity as a "default" religion

Even today the United States of America is a religious country, its society is
deeply rooted in Christian Protestant tradition. When the immigrants came to
America, for them the "default" American religion was Christianity. It was
introduced as "Americanness."

Becoming American was one of the things that the immigrants craved for most
and there was only one American identity, which did not include multiethnic and
multicultural characteristics of immigrants. The school was the first step on the
road to Americanness, and there were compromises to be made.

Mary Antin describes how at school the class said "the Lord's prayer."

"In the middle of the prayer a Jewish boy across the aisle trod on my foot to get
my attention. "You must not say that"..."it's Christian"... I did not know but what
he was right, but the name of Christ was not in the prayer, and I was bound to do
everything that the class did. If I had any Jewish scruples, they were lagging
away behind my interest in school affairs" (165). Michael Gold, Rose Cohen and
Alfred Kazin give accounts of encounters with Christian missionaries who
launched a mighty campaign to convert the Jews. "They set up schools and
orphanages designed in particular to attract Jewish children. They roamed

hospitals and sought deathbed conversions." In schools Christian prayers and mandatory readings of the King James version of the Bible made immigrant children a captive audience of the missionaries (Diner, The Jews, 118-119). Rose Cohen's younger siblings attended school that was connected with a church. When the family had nothing to eat, they are told that "any child in class who would say a prayer received a slice of bread and honey" (Cohen, 160).

Many literary works and memoirs look at Christmas as a symbol of assimilation. In the Jewish consciousness, Christmas and Easter are connected with persecution and pogroms, whereas for Christian America they are the biggest holidays. For Anne Roiphe. "Christmas is a kind of checking point where one can stop and view oneself on the assimilation route" (206). Her mother considered Christmas an American holiday and made sure her children got the best of America. It was a "strange Christmas without a Christ."

Grace Paley deals with this topic in a humorous way when she describes in her short story "The Loudest Voice." how Jewish children are taught the Christian tradition in American schools. Shirley is chosen to participate in a Christmas play because she has a "particularly loud, clear voice with lots of expression" (35). Jewish children are given roles in a Christmas play and the story is retold from a child's point of view. Her parents discuss what is happening at the school: "You're in America! Clara, you wanted to come here. In Palestine the Arabs would be eating you alive. Europe you had pogroms. Argentina is full of Indians. Here you got Christmas...Some joke, ha?" (36).

Christmas is inseparable from America, it comes in one and the same "package" and cannot be disposed of. It is a "creeping pogrom," a thing which brings the assimilation in a "nice" holiday package. The "kind city administration" places a Christmas tree on a street corner. "In order to miss its chilly shadow." the neighbors walk three blocks in the cold to buy the bread, because the tree offends their feelings. It is "a stranger in Egypt" in the predominantly Jewish neighborhoods, and it is a part of "genuine" America. It never would occur to the city administration that their efforts to integrate the new citizens might be offending to their religious feelings, and to the citizens it would never occur to complain -- for them it is inevitable to be a minority whose interests are not taken into account.

In Nathan Englander's short story "Reb Kringle," an Orthodox Jew has a temporary job as a Santa in a chain supermarket store, entertaining children. He is the only one among all Santas who has a genuine beard. He thinks this job is a sin, but his wife makes him do it. He is famous as a star and even the elevator man recognizes him as "that Rabbi Santa." He is sure that "...his very spirit was being challenged, as if God had become sadistic in his test of the human soul." (146) One of the children goes with safety scissors after his beard, he thinks of him as "a little Nazi." He starts talking with the child who expresses a wish for a menorah. Stunned, Izik the Santa finds out from the boy that he is Jewish, not Christian. His response is: "You ask Santa for Chanukah, you get it" (148).

He promises to bring the candles himself. When the child tells him that they are going to Vermont to go to his new father's parents' church, Izik's patience ends. "Church and no Chanukah" is too much. "He grabbed the pompom hanging down form his head and yanked off his hat, revealing a large black yarmulke" (149). A woman faints upon seeing this. The store was just glad to fire him but was afraid because it just had to pay a fine for firing an "HIV Santa", so it would not have the courage to fire a "Reb Santa or Punjabi Santa."

This is the situation in today's America, where minorities are still perceived as minorities, but nobody wants to get into trouble for discriminating them.

1.3 Conversion to Judaism

It seems that the topic of conversion to Judaism is becoming quite common in works of American Jewish literature, though it is not a common phenomenon in Jewish religious life. Judaism is not a proselytizing religion, it does go out to recruit newcomers and does not encourage conversion. Many people would agree with Tova Mirvis's character who is wondering about a convert: "She couldn't understand why anyone would voluntarily take on so many commandments. She had enough trouble remembering all of them and she had been born into it" (Ladies Auxiliary, 90).

Diversity and freedom of choice are highly valued in American culture and Judaism has become one of the choices. Popularity of the conversion theme signifies the new openness of American Christian society. Being American can mean anything, like in Jish Gen's novel <u>Mona in the Promised Land</u>. It is a novel by Chinese-American writer, which deals with Jewish-American issues as one of the central themes. For Jish Gen's heroine, a Chinese-American, being American means being anything she wants. She chooses being Jewish partly because most of her friends are Jewish and she lives in a Jewish neighborhood. Her parents are not happy about her choice. They made a point of telling her that they came to the United States to become American and not Jewish. "Jewish is American... American means being whatever you want, and I happened to pick being Jewish" (Jen, 49).

This ironic exaggeration shows how different today's American culture is from what it used to be, when all immigrants strived to become the "default" white Christian Americans. Now, there is a split in Mona's family – she chooses to become Jewish, her sister is searching for her ancient roots by learning Chinese: all this to dissatisfaction and disapproval of their mother, who wants her children to be American but demands the obedience of a "good Chinese daughter." It is the only thing she does not get from her daughters who are already American, because they make their choices themselves.

Her decision to become Jewish is formed when Mona is tagged along to the Temple Youth activities. She is helping build the Sukka for Sukkot and helps guide tours for some parents "who have never seen a Sukka before, and want to know what it means" (Jen, 32). One of the parents shows concern that their kids are turning too orthodox, returning to the Middle Ages, but she reassures them, "How orthodox can they be...After all, here I am" (33).

But when someone asks her what she is doing here, Mona starts thinking. Then she approaches the Rabbi who gives her the books to read and she starts to learn. She explains that the Chinese are also a minority, "... and if you want to know how to be a minority, there's nobody better at it than the Jews..

You've got to know all the ritual, so you know who you are and don't spend your time trying to be Wasp and acting like you don't have anything to complain about. You've got to realize you're a minority" (Jen, 53, 137). It is not worth trying to be a "mainstream" Wasp so one might as well learn how to be a minority and act accordingly. "Jen's novel might be seen as an end-of-the century status report on the Jewish immigrant experience... more broadly, the novel illustrates the sea change between the immigrant dreams of the past and the immigrant dreams of the present" (Furman, "Immigrant Dreams," 212).

In Tova Mirvis's The Ladies Auxiliary the main character is a convert, who comes to a small Southern community of Memphis, Tennessee after her husband's tragic death. Her name is Batsheva and we never learn her name before the conversion. She wants her daughter to grow up in a close-knit religious community and find an extended family. But everything is not so simple because she is different. She tries to find new spirituality in rituals which became routine for other members of the Orthodox community. She brings a new creative interpretation and tries to find meaning in rituals which are still new to her. She explains: "When I pray or when I eat kosher food, I try to remember that the purpose of my actions is to seek this closeness with God and spirituality" (Mirvis, 49). She wakes curiosity of the community members and is asked questions about her conversion. The Rabbi's wife apologizes for it, thinking to herself that "the Torah says once someone converts, you aren't allowed to single her out and make her feel like a stranger, because we too were once strangers in the land of Egypt" (93). This reflects the traditional Jewish view of conversion, which is not encouraged, but once it is done, a convert is a part of the Jewish people.

Jocelyn, a member of the community who returned to Orthodox Judaism, realizes that she and Batsheva have much in common: "In more ways than Jocelyn liked to admit, this reminded her of her own background. She had grown up with nothing Jewish. Her parents were immigrants anxious to become Americans... With all the teasing she had endured in public school about her parents' accents and old-fashioned clothing, she thought she should at least know what Judaism was about" (Mirvis, 61). Maybe the interest in conversion is connected to interest in return to Judaism, since many people like Jocelyn, who are born Jewish but did not grow up in traditional way, are in many ways similar to converts.

Another modern Jewish-American writer, Tova Reich introduces converts to her novels set in Israel. One of them is Sora Katz in The Master of Return.

> Her name might be Sora Katz now, but there had been a time when she was known to one and all as Pam Buck, and this was a historical fact that Bruria Lurie could never totally assimilate. If the leap from Barbara Horowitz from Brooklyn, New York to Rebbetzin Bruria Lurie of Uman

House was of such breathless magnitude, how much more difficult, perhaps even impossible, was the leap from Pam Buck of Macon, Georgia, to Sora Katz of Mea Shearim, Jerusalem? (Reich, 107)

Sora is the Yiddish pronunciation of Sarah, the foremother of the Jewish people, and also the name which Nazis put after every Jewish name in 1930's Germany. The only way Bruria, who is herself an American immigrant, can explain this metamorphosis is that it is very American to turn into something else. "Why would anyone in his right mind want to become a Jew? You'd have to be crazy, or a masochist, or something...You don't understand Americans. It's deep down there, in her Southern heritage. She's being born again – born-again Christian, born-again Moslem, born-again Jew – what difference does it make to her?" (Reich, 107).

In the <u>Jewish War</u>, the convert is also a former American Christian who, as the rumors go, used to be a stripper in her Gentile life. Incidentally or not, her name is Pam Buck, too. It turns out to be the same person, who moves from one novel to another. The story of her conversion is that   "...due to youthful overexposure to an array of psychiatrists by her... well-meaning mother... the young Pam had developed an early attraction to Jewish types" (Reich, <u>Jewish War,</u> 66). Now she is *rebbetzin* Sora Freud, who belongs to the Anti-Israel sect *The Messiah-Waiters,* "who hold that the establishment of the Jewish State is a sin, an iniquitous interference in God's promise to bring the Messiah in his own time" (Reich, <u>Jewish War</u>, 153).

This is a bitter satire of the ultra-Orthodox groups who are rabidly anti-Israel and who claim that the Zionist State has nothing to do with the religion – it is a plot of secular socialists. According to them only after the Messiah comes is it allowed to settle in the Holy Land. Rebbetzin's brother is a preacher named Chuck Buck, who organizes a conference for repenting Antisemites in Jerusalem. Another convert is Professor Doctor Abraham Ger in <u>Master of the Return.</u> Ger means "convert" in Hebrew.

Reb Lev presents him to the members of his congregation during the Purim celebration:

> And we have here today Professor Dr. Avraham Ger, formerly of Germany, may its name be erased, a convert from the seed of Amalec, from the descendants of Haman, from the most vile anti-Semites in history. No words can express. And now he has become one of us, he has

been detoxified and defanged, he has been turned into a hamantasch, and can no longer do us any harm. To the stranger and the convert we must show no malice, our Torah reaches us. (Reich,162-63)

The convert is "defanged" as if he were a vampire and then turned into a traditional Purim cookie, but still Reb Lev is suspicious:

> Reb Lev had a problem accepting Avraham Ger as an authentic convert, for although Ger had shown the sincerity of his desire to become a Jew by undergoing a circumcision at such a mature age – an experience he had rather enjoyed, according to his own account – his training and preparation for joining the faith had been transacted through the mails, in a
> correspondence course. (175-176)

Reich ridicules the absurdity of hatred between religions and nations, stemming from prejudice and ignorance.

1.4   Substitutes for religion

When the Jewish immigrants came to the United States many of them stopped observing religious rituals. But there were things like education, Holocaust, Anti-Semitism and Israel which gained importance and served as substitutes for the religion.

Judaism is a religion which treasures learning and education. The best match in an Eastern European *stetl* for a rich girl was to marry a Torah scholar who would spend his days learning, while the father of the bride paid for his room and board. Spirituality in Judaism can be achieved by studying the Jewish religious texts, the Talmud.   For immigrant Jews education was the most important asset. Their access to secular learning was limited in tsarist Russia, where it was almost impossible for a Jew to secure a place at a university if he or she did not want to convert.

For early immigrant writers like Abraham Cahan, Anzja Yezierska and Mary Antin the new religion is education. Their temples are libraries and universities. Education is their god. For David Levinsky a college is a symbol of spirituality. "My old religion had gradually fallen to pieces ...church-like structure...was the synagogue of my new life. Nor is this merely a figure of speech: the building really appealed to me as a temple, as a House of Sanctity, as we call the ancient Temple of Jerusalem" (Cahan, 169).

His Temple is destroyed when the dream of higher education fades away.

"The college building was a source of consolation. Indeed, what was money beside the halo of higher education?" (Cahan, 80).

Mary Antin describes the public library as a place "even better than school in some ways" (201). "It was my habit to go very slowly up the low, broad steps to the palace entrance, pleasing my eyes with the majestic lines of the building, and lingering to read again the carved inscriptions Public library - Built by the People- Free to All" (266).

After the World War II, the only connection of many modern Jews to Judaism was the Holocaust. In a way it became a substitute for a religious experience. It is especially relevant in America, where many descendants of immigrants did not have a thorough Jewish upbringing, and their only notion of Judaism was persecution, suffering and the Final Solution.

It is reflected in many works of fiction by Jewish writers who did not have the firsthand experience but who identified themselves with the victims.

Ezra Cappell mentions Arthur Cohen's remark that American Jews are the Holocaust witnesses who "bear the scar without the wound" (108).

The principle of equality which is the essence of American democracy is inverted and passed onto the Jews who were murdered without exception.

Erica Jong wrote the following definition of being Jewish: " A Jew is a person who can convert to Christianity from now to Doomsday, and still be killed by Hitler if his mother was Jewish" (Who We Are, 101).

Tova Reich expresses the thought that all Jews no matter what their convictions and social class are all connected through the Shoah. After ridiculing almost every Jewish and non-Jewish group and movement in her book, she becomes very serious.

> ...every single type of Jew without exception was hunted down...no Jew was excused...no Jew could any longer reasonably claim to be superior to another...we must love and identify with all Jews because, in the end, all Jews are created equal, as they say in America, at any moment we Jews might find ourselves herded together without discrimination in the same cattle car, or packed naked together without distinction in the same gas chamber, our nameless ashes mixed up randomly together in the same great ash heap. (Reich, Jewish War, 257)

The Jewish State became another "substitute" for religion as more and more young Jewish Americans identified themselves with Israel's fight for survival, and felt proud for their Jewish identity after the glorious victory following the Six Day War, when they realized that being Jewish does not only mean being a victim but also a heroic pioneer warrior, rebuilding the land of the forefathers. For many Jews today the State of Israel plays the central role in their identity as Jews, inevitably entering Jewish literary works. Jewish citizens living outside of Israel have a problem of double allegiance to Israel and their respective country. In America, the Bible rhetoric of a "promised land" is used by Protestant majority. For many Jews, America became a "promised land" as well, a shelter and a safe haven after centuries of religious persecution. There is a "competition" between the historical and biblical "promised land" of Israel and the American "promised land" of individual pursuit of private happiness and individual goals. Sometimes there is a serious dilemma, when an American Jew has to decide which one of the promised lands has a priority. Although both countries are close allies, it is not always an easy decision.

1.5 Antisemitism

Antisemitism is a part of Jewish experience, something that is inevitable and ubiquitous, one has to put up with it. It has its roots in the religious dispute between world's monotheistic religions, every one of them claiming the exclusive rights on the true godly revelation. The Christian Church, which claimed to be "the New Israel" and to have overtaken the "birthright" of the Chosen People, claimed that the Jews killed Jesus and as a punishment were sent to suffer in exile.

Immigrant writers tend to describe the Old World Anti-Semitism that they escaped from. Mary Antin describes the situation in her native town, where the Jewish and Gentile populations were segregated and had no contact with each other. The Jews lived in the Pale, they could not move freely in the country and could not live in big cities with very few exceptions. "The world was divided into Jews and Gentiles... It was the priests...who taught people to hate the Jews" (Antin, 8). She graphically describes the horrible pogroms: "They [the peasants] attacked them [the Jews] with knives and clubs and scythes and axes, killed them or tortured them, and burned their houses. This was called a "pogrom"...Only to hear these things made one sob and sob and choke with pain" (10). For Antin, Antisemitism with its horrors stayed in the old World. In America, she knows no segregation between Jews and Gentiles. The Jews are not discriminated against if they agree to assimilate. Her speech at the Protestant church, on one of her tours in Vermont, symbolizes the victory of universalism, the goal and outcome of which is full assimilation. "Centuries of Jewish history are atoned for in this moment...The dark abyss of separation between Jew and Gentile is closed by my presence in this pulpit" (Sollors, Introduction, XLIX).

As a logical consequence there is no need to stay Jewish, if there is no Antisemitism. The Judaism is forced upon a person by the hostile outside world like a mark of Cain. The associations with Judaism are purely negative.

When the hostility stops, one can interact, eat and intermarry with the Gentiles. To keep one's Judaism is not necessary anymore, it becomes redundant.

Antin is sorry about it in a way: "And yet if the golden truth of Judaism had not been handed me in the motley rags of formalism, I might not have been so ready to put away my religion" (Antin, 190). She foresees almost with a prophetic vision that things will change:

> My grandchildren, for all I know, may have a graver task than I have set them. Perhaps they may have to testify that the faith of Israel is a heritage that no heir in the direct line has the power to alienate form his successors. Even I, with my limited perspective, think it doubtful if the conversion of the Jew to any alien belief or disbelief is ever thoroughly accomplished. What positive affirmation of the persistence of Judaism in the blood my descendants may have to make, I may not be present to hear. (195)

Sometimes a completely assimilated Jew finds his or her way back to Judaism because of Antisemitism. A typical example is Philip Roth's character in Counterlife, who feels Jewish because of his wife's family's Antisemitism.

When he accompanies his wife to Church on Christmas he feels his Jewishness, which is otherwise not a meaningful part of his identity.

> It never fails. I am never more of a Jew than I am in a church when the organ begins. I may be estranged at the Wailing Wall but without being a stranger – I stand outside but not shut out, and even the most ludicrous or

hopeless encounter serves to gauge, rather than sever, my affiliation with people I couldn't be less like. But between me and church devotion there is an unbridgeable world of feeling, a natural and thouroughgoing incompatibility - I have the emotions of a spy in the adversary's camp and feel I'm overseeing the very rites that embody the ideology that's been responsible for the persecution and mistreatment of Jews." (Roth, Counterlife, 256)

The knowledge of history of persecution of the Jewish people makes the protagonist identify himself with the persecuted and feel his difference.

Marge Piercy's character Shira in He She and It feels she is "too loud, too female, too Jewish, too dark, too exuberant, too emotional" in the corporate world of her multi. She feels herself as "other" because she sees herself through the eyes of the "other", it is Anti-Semitism internalized. Similar thing happens to David Levinsky when he is worried that his excessive gesticulation might make his Gentile companions despise him. The desire to get rid of identity markers, to assimilate, to fit in, to be Americanized as soon as possible is a response to Anti-Semitism which exists in American society albeit on a different level.

J.S. Foyer, who is a third-generation writer, describes his encounters with Anti-Semitism while visiting Ukraine. Though it is presented in an absurdly funny way, one realizes it is felt on everyday level. He describes an encounter with a waitress. She is interested in the American tourist and when told by his translator that he is a Jew, she says :"I have never seen a Jew before. Can I see his horns?" (Foyer, 107). This would be hilarious if it weren't so sad at the same time.

The narrator, Alexandr Perchov is a Ukrainian who works as a translator in an agency called "Heritage Touring" which works for "...the Jews, who try to unearth places where their families once existed" (3).

He is deeply surprised when he sees his American friend for the first time. "When we found each other I was very flabbergasted by his appearance. This is an American? I thought. This is a Jew? He was severely short... He did not appear like either the Americans I had witnessed in magazines, with yellow hairs and muscles, or the Jews from history books, with no hairs and prominent bones. He was wearing nor blue jeans nor the uniform" (Foyer, 32).

The stereotypes that Alexandr has of the Jews stem from the Nazi propaganda books, and the stereotypes of Americans from the Soviet propaganda books.

When he for the first time sees a living person who represents both stereotypes, he is very confused.

But America is also not immune to Anti-Semitism. Marge Piercy describes in her autobiography Sleeping with Cats the Anti-Semitism of her family in America, she and her mother are Jewish and her father is Christian.

> My father's family was casually and relentlessly anti-Semitic, so neither my mother nor I was ever easy with them...We were always being observed to see if we would do something Jewish like crucify somebody in the backyard. If my mother or I ever laughed, or raised our voices, or used our hands in talking, there was a look that would pass between them that would silence us...They never missed an opportunity to serve ham to us." (Piercy, Sleeping with Cats, 20)

They are put under scrutiny, insulted and excluded, ritually forbidden food is served to them as an additional insult.

Tova Reich targets American Anti-Semitism in her merciless satire of the Christian groups who support Israel. She depicts a confession at a Christian conference in Israel. It is organized by an American Christian named Chuck Buck, who meets the main character Yehudi Ha-Goel and calls him "brother Jew-dee, alluding to the common Jewish name "Yehuda" which has several meanings: one is simply "a Jew," "Judea" in Hebrew, one of the twelve brothers – the tribes of Israel, and for a Christian ear it also reminds of Judas – the traitor of Jesus according to the New Testament.

> The faithful are scheduled to gather and rise up...to confess in merciless and unsparing detail, their sins of anti-semitism, their anti-semitic thoughts and deeds of the past...they will beg forgiveness on bended knees of the Jewish people, whom they have slandered, maligned, injured, and plain murdered, and they will consecrate the remainder of their days on earth to the well-being of the Jewish State upon which heir own salvation and redemption are eternally dependent. (Reich, Jewish War, 149)

Reich is bitter in her grotesque and surreal account of a woman, who "was confessing, how...she used to be allergic to Jews...she had a certified medical allergy to Jews, it was a physical thing with her that could not be helped, just the thought of a Jew, not to mention a Jew's physical presence would cause her to break out in rashes all over her body" (162). The Anti-Semitism as a disease inverts the notion of a "Jewish disease," the state of "incurable Jewishness."

The woman finds a doctor in Bethlehem, Pennsylvania, the name of the birth place of Jesus, which is duplicated on American continent. It refers to the Christian notion of taking on the role of the chosen people from the Jews who rejected the Christian Messiah. The doctor helps the woman by taking "a bit of extract-of-Jew that he had in a vial in his cabinet... every two weeks or so she got her shots of two cubic centimeters of Jew venom-- a mixture of lechery, niggardliness, opportunism, haughtiness, finagling, haggling, sycophancy, ugliness, treachery, pushiness, casuistry, etc. etc...her allergy to Jews became her career, her life's work..." (163-164). Finally her allergies stopped and she came all the way to Jerusalem to beg forgiveness of the Jewish people.

The theme of Anti-Semitism is no less relevant today than it was in Mary Antin's generation, and Jewish American authors deal with it in their works of fiction on different levels. If immigrant writers thought that assimilating would redeem them from the plague of "otherness," blaming themselves for being different, modern authors often take satirical approach and put the blame on those who are prejudiced and not on those who are suffering from these prejudices.

2. Religious sources

The use of Jewish sources ranging from the Bible, classical rabbinical *hagaddic* and *halachic* material and liturgy is finding its way to the pages of modern novels. An example of such a source is the *Midrash*. *Midrash* means "interpretation" or "exegesis" in Hebrew. It is a classical rabbinical story providing a commentary on the Bible or a legend, a fantastic elaboration on a Bible story. According to David Zucker, modern authors turned to these texts, integrating them into their works and offering them new levels of meaning. "The act of echoing, interacting, and interpenetrating with past texts has a venerable history in Judaism" (7). In the Talmud, the page is built around a certain passage where a commentary upon commentary is written. Modern writers write their own "commentary" on biblical or rabbinic stories. Zucker notes that authors place characters in a modern-day setting but sometimes use material from the rabbinic past. Intertextuality is a typical feature of the Jewish traditional and also of secular writing.

Tova Reich uses many different religious sources in her novels. For instance in Master of the Return, *Midrash Rabbah* on Exodus (26. II --10), is a story of how Moses became a stutterer that is told by Abba Nisim to Akiva, the main character's child (196). It evokes a classical situation in Jewish tradition, when learning is passed from a father to a son. Another Midrash used in the novel is the story of accepting the Torah by the Jewish people at Mount Sinai. Direct biblical sources are also often used or alluded to. Dara Horn paraphrases the Book of Job in one the chapters titled "The Book of Hurricane Job" in her novel In the Image. She uses poetic language which is associated with the Bible. Her characters are called "Leora the New Jerseyite" and "Yehuda the Brooklynite," places in America which became parts of the Jewish history and tradition.

In Reich's Master of the Return, Ivriya Himmelhoch begs God to give her back her lost child by means of a note tucked into the Wailing Wall. It alludes to the Psalm 118: "She wrote: Into this cranny Ivriya bat Frieda inserts herself. From the straits she cried out to You. She begs You to answer her, in the breadth of Your generosity. Ivriya bat Frieda is asking for pity: pity her, pity her. Oh, pity me!" (233). The beginning of the note is written in a third person, but she ends it with a first person appealing to God. She finds her direct path to God in time of need, without intermediaries. The response letter received by regular mail has a word order which sounds like a "direct translation" from Hebrew: "To the Widow, Ivriya bat Frieda, Greetings! ...Regarding your appeal from the "straits" ...you have failed to keep in mind the noble words of the holy Rav Nahman, that the entire world is an exceedingly narrow bridge, and the essential thing is not to be afraid" (Reich, 233). She uses here a line out of a famous folk song ascribed to Rav Nachman of Bratslav, who is one of the most important characters in the novel. This song is very popular, its English translation is:

> The whole world
> is a very narrow bridge
> a very narrow bridge
> a very narrow bridge
> And the main thing to recall -
> is not to be afraid.

The letter compares the destruction of Rabbi Nachman's grave in Uman, Ukraine, to the story of the destruction of the Holy Temple in Jerusalem by the Romans.

The holy Temple was turned into a dump and the holy grave was turned into a public toilet. Akiva the boy laughed just like his namesake, the great scholar Rabbi Akiva. The letter uses the story from Talmud, *Masechet Makot* 24 a,b.

> ... Rabbi Akiva, when he walked among the ruins of the Temple Mount and viewed foxes emerging from the Holy of Holies. His companions, Rabban Gamliel, Rabbi Eleazer ben Azariah, and Rabbi Joshua, wept at the sight, just as I wept at Uman, but Rabbi Akiva was merry, for in the destruction he was witnessing he recognized the fulfillment of the first stage of the prophesy, and this, in turn, signified the imminent realization of the second phase, the rebuilding of the holy city of Jerusalem. (Reich, Master of the Return, 234)

Ivriya is compared to the foremother Rachel who, in the Jewish tradition, is weeping for her children, alluding to Jeremiah: "A voice is heard in Ramah, Lamentation and bitter weeping. Rachel is weeping for her children; She refuses to be comforted for her children, Because they are no more" (New American Standard Bible, Jer. 31.15). "Mother Rachel, let your tears flow no more. Your hope will be fulfilled. Your children will return" (Reich, 235).

It refers also a famous folk song sung on the 9th of Av, the fast day to commemorate the destruction of the First and the Second Temple in Jerusalem.

The demands on the reader are very high, the writer assumes that the reader would understand the intertextual references.

Sanford Pinsker notes that Reich's novels:" make heavy demands on their readers. One needs to know a good deal about Hasidism..." (qtd in Meyer, 117).

Tova Mirvis also quotes religious sources extensively in her novel The Outside World. In a paragraph where Baruch – Brian puts on his phylacteries there is a quote from Exodus 13:9, which refers to this commandment: "And it shall be as a sign to you on your hand and a memorial between you eyes" (Mirvis, 29).

This parallel helps understand the idea of a connection between the character's development to become more strictly orthodox and the religious sources which inspire him for that. It makes an ironic impression because it makes the reader realize how literally Brian takes everything and that he follows the religious injunctions without thinking twice. Other quotes in this scene are from Leviticus,

Joshua and *Shulchan Aruch* (a book of religious laws for everyday life).

> Jet lag and laziness had conspired against him, and he had slept late, through minyan at shul, which he was commanded by God to attend ("He should not separate himself from the congregation when they pray" - Shulhan Aruch 90). Before he left yeshiva, his rabbi had warned him against being lulled into the complacency of his parents' so-called Modern Orthodox world ("You shall not walk in the ways of the other nations" - Leviticus 18:4). Five days in America and this was what had happened... After davening, Baruch had sat in the beis midrash, the yeshiva's book-lined study hall, and learned Talmud...At night, he returned to the beis midrash to review the pages that had been covered during the day ("And you shall be occupied with it day and night"- Joshua 1:8). (Mirvis, 29-30)

The words which Mirvis does not explain – like *davening, minyan*, and *shul* – a prayer, a religious quorum necessary for prayer of ten men, and synagogue – are accessible only to readers who possess Jewish religious knowledge.

All the quotes are in English, connecting them to the Puritan Christian tradition.

Another source of traditional material is liturgy. Often authors use traditional prayers which would be known to a Jewish reader sometimes in transliteration, sometimes in translation. For instance Tova Reich uses a prayer from the traditional prayer book in <u>Master of the Return.</u> It is quoted in English translation :"It is our duty to praise the Master of All, to exalt the Creator of Universe..." (205). Dara Horn has her main character in <u>In the Image</u> open a box of phylacteries which contains a scroll with the most important Jewish prayer, "Hear O Israel", which is quoted in the text.

One of the most common prayers used in many works of American Jewish fiction is *Kaddish.* Hana Wirth-Nesher notes that Kaddish – an Aramaic prayer for the dead is used as a marker of Jewish identity. "Kaddish" means "sanctification" in Aramaic and it is a prayer expressing faith in Israel's messianic redemption. Originally, the Kaddish had nothing to do with bereavement, it was a formula with which all synagogue services concluded. Kaddish is believed to have originated in Babylon when the vernacular of the Jews used to be Aramaic. Today a son is obligated to say Kaddish for eleven months of mourning (this time period believed to be the maximum period when the soul of the deceased is undergoing a cleansing process). Daughters are prohibited from reciting it and the traditional gender restrictions call attention to the prayer as a symbol of exclusion of women from religious practice. (Wirth-Nesher, Liturgy, 116). Wirth-Nesher defines Kaddish as "antithesis" of Passover Seder. It is also an act of remembering but not of a whole nation; it remembers the soul of one single person (121).

Kaddish is invoked in Jewish American literature for a number of reasons, like its rhythm and cadence, content which can be interpreted as praise for individual human beings rather than God, and its performative aspect as prayer for the dead, which is connected to the Holocaust and serves a sign of mourning for extinguished Jewish life of prewar Europe. Kaddish almost always appears in transliteration, because even the most of religious Jewish readers would not be able to read it in Hebrew alphabet but are familiar with the sound of the transliterated prayer which evokes certain associations and reminds of their religious experience (Wirth-Nesher, Liturgy,124).

I think it corresponds with the idea of the Holocaust, as sometimes the only remaining connection to Judaism, and the Kaddish is the only vestige of one's Jewish observance.

...Jewish American fiction has tended to treat the Kaddish as a signifier of the "essence" of Judaism or Jewishness, as a ritual untouched by the processes of assimilation or accommodation. The eruption of the Kaddish into so many Jewish American works of literature is usually not a sign of the theological, of the transcendent or the divine, but rather an affirmation of the continuity of Israel based on immanence, within history. (Wirth-Nesher, 122)

The paradox of the use Kaddish is that it is a marker of Jewish self-identification and religious identity, affirming continuity because one needs a Jewish son to recite Kaddish for (in Yiddish culture, a son was humorously called "my Kaddish") through a ritual connected with death. "...the proliferation of the Kaddish in Jewish American literature after the Second World War may be a response both to the Holocaust and to assimilation, as the act of mourning becomes an essential aspect of Jewish American identity" (Liturgy, 128).

It seems that the stories of the post-war period portray acts of mourning, as if the act of mourning itself were the ultimate Jewish marker. Books which have appeared in the past two decades blend the mourning and the praise, thus looking back and also looking forward to the future (128).

I agree with Hana Wirth-Nesher, and think that the finding of new hope and simultaneous return to the roots through religious revival can be seen as a general development in the latest literary works. It is a revival which does not exclude women anymore, who are also present at reciting the Kaddish as equals.

The aspirations of the new generation of writers are maybe best expressed by Dara Horn who is a doctoral candidate in comparative literature at Harvard University studying Hebrew and Yiddish. In an interview about her book, In the Image, she said she was inspired by modern Hebrew and Yiddish literature, particularly early modern writers, who constantly refer to the Hebrew Bible and commentaries, even while challenging the religious tradition. She wonders if it is possible to create this sort of literature in English, using biblically anchored language within a secular text. She realized that English readers are familiar with biblical literature only in archaic translations. "This made it possible to create a work in English that could be read on several levels... I wanted to create a different style for American Jewish literature, one more connected to the Jewish literary tradition of constant reference to ancient text." (Horn, Interview).

2.1 Folklore and mysticism: Golem and reincarnation

One of the most popular tropes used in modern American Jewish fiction is Golem. It is a figure from Jewish folklore, an artificial being - usually, although not always, male, made mostly of clay by a man using the magic of the Kabbalah. The Hebrew word "Golem" literally means "a shapeless or lifeless matter" (Morris, 1).

According to Ruth Bienstock Anolik, a golem is created for practical purposes, often to be a saviour of innocent people. Usually the golem ultimately evades the control of its creator. The Golem stories are found in ancient rabbinic and cabbalistic texts and also in 17th, 18th, and 19th century texts which are based on the earlier tradition. These stories originated in supernatural tales of rabbinic literature and became part of the folk tale tradition ("Reviving the Golem", 37). The Golem figure has entered today's popular American culture in a number of ways ranging from literary works to the comics.

According to Anolick, the female Jewish writers' feminism is transforming the golem tradition in contemporary writing. Jewish women have become a part of a tradition in which the highest aspiration of a religious person is to be a scholar. At the same time, it is a tradition that had usually limited women's access to learning.

In the Talmudic culture, the word golem which also means "unformed substance" is associated with women, especially unmarried or barren. As in many ancient cultures, Jewish women are not seen as separate beings, they are a part of their families, their husbands or fathers. Just like the golem is speechless and cannot participate fully in religious life, so must women be. It is known that the access to Kabbala was traditionally allowed only to married males over the age of forty. Anolik reminds that even the access to language which is the main tool of creation was limited.

Cynthia Ozick and Marge Piercy appropriate and transform the figure of Golem in their writing and open a space for a creative and powerful woman who procreates by intellectual will and does not need a male protective figure in her life. Marge Piercy's Golem -- Cyborg Yod in He, She and It, is created as a male by a man, but, as his name suggests to readers who speak Hebrew, he is a tenth model after nine failures who tended to be violent. Only after his creator Avram invites a woman programmer to help "program" or rather socialize the cyborg, does he succeed in creating a model which becomes successful.

In Cynthia Ozick's "Puttermesser and Xantippe" from The Puttermesser Papers, a female protagonist creates a female golem. In the Jewish tradition only male scholars create golems because to be a scholar is a male prerogative. Ozick tells a story of a mother-daughter relationship which is based on a traditionally male tale. Puttermesser is an unmarried lawyer and civil servant of forty-six. Ozick is somewhat ironic about her feminist views and political correctness. She is a feminist who is careful about her pronouns: "She always said "humankind" instead of "mankind." She always wrote "he or she" instead of just "he"(Ozick, 24). It seems her feminism on paper is hardly to be taken seriously, but it is an important detail because in the Jewish tradition words have a power to destroy and create and in this particular case words give and take life.

Puttermesser longs to be a mother – like a "normal" Jewish girl should. "She imagined daughters" but her desire is selfish because "all these daughters were Puttermesser as a child" (Ozick, 36). Her golem daughter is a copy of her would-be wild self, it is an attempt to regain the lost childhood.

Elaine Kaviar thinks that Puttermesser's regret over her lost childhood is connected to her desire to own a past. Her imaginary uncle Zindel who teaches her Hebrew is an attempt to claim an ancestor who connects her to her Jewish roots (40-42). The creation of golem is connected to the Jewish tradition which is rooted in the past.

Puttermesser wants to be proud of her would-be daughter, who would study Latin and German like her mother. Her imaginary daughter chants at first Virgil and Catullus in Latin, then, still in high school, memorizes Goethe's *Erlkoenig* in German. After hearing the imaginary "In seinen Armen das Kind war tot," Puttermesser wants to sob. She buries the imaginary child, who is dead in two languages, first in Latin, the language of the high culture and the Roman conquerors of Judea, and then in German, the language also associated with high culture and the Third Reich. Hebrew is a revelation for her: "...she whose intellectual passions were pledged to every alphabet... a single primeval Hebrew word, shimmering with its lightning holiness, the Name of Names..." (40).

The Hebrew letters stand out in an English text, although the word itself is not named, it means only "the name" in Hebrew, which stands for the name of God in order not to utter it in vain when one is not praying or studying religious texts . One word in Hebrew has so much weight that it makes a dead body come to life. Puttermesser is shocked upon discovering a dirty body in her high-minded civilized bed. Puttermesser had no intention to create a golem and does it seemingly by accident. Instead of giving birth like a regular woman, Puttermesser creates life by words, in the tradition of male scholars. Elaine Kauvar notes that the connection between ideas and children is made by Socrates when he describes ideas as the "offsprings of one's soul" (43). Puttermesser prefers reading Socrates to lovemaking and her soul's offspring is a golem.

But her creation, Lea-Xanthippe, is female. Lust for a man, the danger of unleashed sexuality which wins over rational thinking is what undoes the golem in the end of the story. Her "daughter" turns out to be literate in all languages "All tongues are mine, especially that of my mother,"(41) but she cannot speak. Which is the "tongue of my mother" is unclear - is it Hebrew, which was used for her creation, or English, or Yiddish, or maybe Latin or German?

Ozick's Golem is very modern and very American – the old Golem legend is transferred to American soil and transformed. The golem chooses her name by herself and she wants no Hebrew name of Lea. She wants to be called according to her own taste – Xanthippe, after Socrates' wife. It reminds the reader that Socrates had both intellectual and personal life, which Puttermesser, as a female, cannot have. In order to be able to pursue her intellectual aspirations she had to banish her lover who was distracting her. In this way she can never be an equal to a male scholar. Miriam Sivan thinks that "...Xanthippe rejects, along with her Hebrew name, a guiding moral code. She is devoted to her "mother's" mission until she has had a taste of the erotic in life. It is a fruit doubly forbidden to her, for a golem traditionally lacks two essential components of a human being: speech and a sex drive"(99).

After saying "I hear and obey," like the Jewish people on Mount Sinai according to a *midrash*, the next word she writes is a "no." She advertises herself – "now watch me walk" and is trying to bargain with her creator: "I will be of use to you. Don't send me away" (42). Xanthippe wants to be first in everything like a true American. She claims to be the first female golem. When Puttermesser tells her about Ibn Gabirol's creation, a female golem, made not of clay but of wood and hinges with the goal to be her creator's companion and housekeeper, Lea dismisses it by proclaiming: "that was not a true golem"(43). Xanthippe cannot speak but has her own ideas and expresses them in writing. She intends to turn New York into paradise. The messianic idea of salvation for the whole population at once is transferred from the Bible to New York.

At the beginning of the story she is called "the thing" or "the creature" – like a soulless, sexless object; then "the golem" and towards the end of the story by her name. The new American feminist golem is in pursuit of her own liberty and happiness abandoning her primary golem's tasks of serving her creator. She is not satisfied long with the position of a "wife" – a domestic servant, into which Puttermesser turns her at first. The chapter name is "The golem cooks, cleans and shops" which is a stereotypical "female" activity. But Xantippe wants more than that, she wants to prove her capabilities. She helps Puttermesser become a mayor thus helping her enter another area of male dominance, where Puttermesser was discriminated both as a woman and a Jew.

The female golem in Ozick's book may be read as a reflection upon the traditional immigrant or Jewish American woman in America. All she does are typical housewife activities, and she is also silent—as if not given the right to voice her opinions. So, in a way, the destruction of the golem at the final scene may be seen as a failure of golem's/woman's emancipation from the restriction of Jewish male-dominated tradition.

Ozick's Puttermesser is careful about the dietary sensitivities of the golem – being what she is, "...Puttermesser sent the golem out to a delicatessen for sandwiches; it was a kosher delicatessen – Puttermesser thought the golem would care about a thing like that" (Ozick, 57). Since the Golem is connected to the Jewish tradition, Puttermesser assumes she would not eat anything improper, though she cares less about other sensitivities of her newly created daughter, making her work as a domestic help. But caring for what she eats becomes a step towards recognition, after Puttermesser took Xantippe to her office and let her type. Xanthippe has a mystical connection to the Ghetto of the Lower East Side. It is a mystical coincidence that her first shopping spree takes place on Delancey street, where she buys a tasteless lamp in the form of the Statue of Liberty, the Statue being the first thing immigrants saw when arriving to the Land of Freedom. "The thronged Caribbean faces and tongues of the Lower East Side drew her; Xanthippe, a kind of foreigner herself...was attracted to immigrant populations. Their tastes and adorations were hers" (Ozick, 59). Golem imagery is associated with the immigrant discourse.

Gershom Sholem explains that the idea of Golem in Judaism is joined to the ideas of creative power of speech and letters. In creating a golem its creator had participated in the ritual of initiation, to which was attached the symbolism of rebirth, the idea being that a golem was buried in the earth from which it rose. (qtd in Kauvar, 43). The idea of immigrant's rebirth goes back to Mary Antin's famous first sentence:"I was born, I have lived, and I have been made over." After the arrival an immigrant is mute as a golem and gradually gains the power of speech.

When Puttermesser becomes mayor and the work of "reformation, reinvigoration and redemption" of the city starts, the golem is sent out to the city. At first, she tends to go to the Lower East Side, but Puttermesser "upbraids her for parochialism" (75). The justice means also equality for everyone – the golem is instructed to take buses and subways – no taxis, like she is prone to do. According to Ozick, the messianic idea of justice and redemption for all humankind is universal – it works for both Jews and Gentiles.

It can be also read as the spreading of Jewish ideas and culture from the immigrant ghetto to the mainstream American world through a story or a literary figure. Xanthippe also longs for daughters she can never have. "A golem cannot procreate! But it has the will to; the despairing will, the violent will. Offspring! Progeny!...Xanthippe, like Puttermesser herself, longs for daughters! Daughters that can never be!" (88). In America, nothing is impossible: even golems have personal wills and desires. In the end she starts speaking – pleading for mercy, imploring not to destroy her. But it is too late. Like in traditional golem stories, Xanthippe resists the power of her creator and has to be returned to clay.

The golem has to be "dismantled," the name has to be erased. The word "dismantle" returns the golem to her "dehumanized" state.

According to Kauvar, the creation of golem confirmed man in his likeness to God and at the same time warned him against idolatry with the letters written on the golem's forehead. The erasure of the letter *alef* from the word *emeth* (truth) left the word *met* (dead) which returned the golem to clay in an act symbolic of a human creator's limitations (44). Puttermesser's ex-lover Rappoport erases the aleph from the golem's forehead. It looks like an old scar – "queerly in the shape of a sort of letter K" (99). Xanthippe is so "Americanized" that her Hebrew letters "assimilated" into half-forgotten scars. The first letter of the word "truth" – *aleph* ("א") is almost impossible to read, it looks like a Latin letter "K" and also X, which is the first letter of Xanthippe's name. Many assimilated Jews only return to their "true Hebrew letters" when they die and Kaddish is recited, evoking the old scars of the Jewish suffering, often in transcription, because their children know only Latin letters. The golem is returned to clay and what is left of her is buried in the City Hall Park. The Americanized Jewish legend is a rejected tale which is transplanted into American soil. Just like Prague, where the original Golem legend was buried, New York has become a part of Jewish folklore.

Ruth Anolik points out that "in creating the first female golem, Puttermesser takes possession of the ancient mystical power of the rabbis, which was historically the domain of male scholars" (39). The golem takes a role of a messiah which is also a traditionally male role. The original golem tales are birth narratives from which mothers are absent. It is the continuation of biblical narratives where only male descendants are named. Other than the gender, Ozick remains faithful to the original story, the structure remains intact and the technologies of creation are exact replica of the methodologies used by rabbis in the folklore tales. "In Ozick's formulation, the feminist project is not to change social and cultural paradigms, but simply to allow women to enter the structures as they are" (39). According to Anolik, Ozick appears to share the traditional Jewish anxieties toward unbridled female sexuality. Puttermesser exists within a narrative and cultural context developed by a male tradition and is a symbol of female self-destruction where Puttermesser is once again powerless and marginalized.

It seems to me though, that Puttermesser herself is the one who decides to destroy her creation, because it threatens the city she loves so much.
Female sexuality is the factor which is traditionally the reason why women are not allowed to study. Their gender prevents them from controlling themselves. I think Ozick tries to imagine what would happen if women became like men in every sphere? This could have fatal consequences for the world.
Puttermesser is the ultimate intellectual woman who prefers reading Plato to making love. Xantippe is the fruit of her brain, not her womb. It is an unnatural product that threatens to destroy the world order. She has to be returned to clay.

Shalom Auslander uses the Golem in a satirical short story It Ain't Easy Bein' Supremey. The main character named Epstein uses the latest edition of *Kabbalah for Dummies* to create a household Golem. Auslander uses a familiar thing like the "for Dummies" series to create a comic effect. After commanding the first golem to stand up and sit, Epstein's mother commands it to do the laundry. This is where the trouble begins. The Golem asks:"Hanging or folded?" Next task is when Epstein commands the Golem to "bring unto him" a beer. The Golem needs the detailed "commandment" in order to fulfill it. "Dost thou desire a Beck's or dost Thou desire a Samuel Adams?" (Auslander, 179). He goes on asking: light or regular, ale or lager, Amber or Cheery Wheat – this goes on until Epstein loses patience. Auslander is well familiar with a kind of a rabbinical dispute this discussion reminds of, where exaggerated attention is given to seemingly unimportant details concerning the religious laws in mundane things. Soon the Golem has thick black notebooks, seven of them are filled from cover to cover, an entire volume on beer, two on the complex subject of chips and related snacks, which is another parody on Talmud.

The hilarious effect is increased by using the archaic language, which is supposed to be similar to the biblical language. Of course, the Talmud and Kabbala languages, in which Golems are "usually" created are Hebrew and Aramaic, not English. The story of the Golem creation was that Epstein, a low-level assistant in a big corporation, felt the need to be significant and to be taken care of. After the Rabbi of his congregation mentioned the story of the Golem of Prague in his Shabbat sermon, "by Saturday night, Epstein was already scouring the Golem section in the local Barnes & Noble (it's not in Sci-Fi, by the way, it's in Biography)" (Auslander,181). Auslander gives a useful tip in which section of the store to look for those of his readers who are eager to try emulating Epstein.

The story is interspersed with quotes from the Book of Psalms where the "Lord" is substituted for "Epstein." For the Golems Epstein is their Creator. Psalm 95 is paraphrased in the first lines of the story:"Come! Let us now sing out to Epstein! Let us call out in praise to the Rock of Salvation! Let me greet him with thanksgiving with praiseful songs let me pray to him, For a great God is Epstein, and a great King above all!" (Auslander, 177). Another paraphrase is Psalm 23: "Epstein is my shepherd, I shall not lack... I shall dwell in the house of Epstein for all my days." (180). Epstein liked that "beseech part."
"Nobody beseeched him at work. Nobody praised him. Nobody sanctified his name." (182). After a few more trips to the Home Depot Garden Center – another "typically" American landmark – Epstein creates Golem Two. He even does the in-your-own-image thing, though *Kabbala for Dummies* advises against it. The results are catastrophic: the plants are not watered, the cat is not fed and the garbage is not taken out, because the golems are in "constant debate about the meaning, intricacies and inferences of Epstein's instructions and commands" (186).

The hilarious effect is strengthened by the details of these discussions, where golems cite passages from Notebook 4, page 42 on Laws concerning the taking out of garbage, which remind of the discussions in legal parts of the Talmud. Epstein goes to consult the Rabbi only to find out that he also has the same Golem problem. His golem also paraphrases the Psalm 23 – in this case substituting the Lord's name for Teitelbaum – the Rabbi's name. The problem is that the "Kabbala for Dummies" gives detailed instructions how to create a golem but not how to uncreate one. The story does not have a happy ending. The golems almost kill each other while arguing over the intricacies of watering the plants. In the battle one loses his legs, another his arms. Epstein has to wash, clothe, feed and carry the disabled Golems around. Epstein becomes their servant and caretaker, the situation is reversed. In the end, the Epsteins have to flee in the night. The Golems call out for Epstein mornings, afternoons and evenings, write notes on pieces of paper begging for forgiveness and salvation, sticking them into the cracks between the bricks in the living room wall. This is an allusion to the remains of the Western Wall of Jerusalem Temple, which is holiest religious site in Judaism. The Western Wall evokes awe and trepidation in the heart of even a non-observant Jew. Trivializing it verges on sacrilege but is at the same time hilarious. The story ends with the sight of destruction: the last of the plants died, the cat starved, and the garbage piled high on the floor.

This story uses Golem trope to mock the religious beliefs, making fun of the rules and rituals. A religious human being is likened to a Golem, which does not have a free will but is created to carry out the will of its master.

The text is rejecting the Jewish religious tradition but is at the same time deeply rooted in it, expecting the same from the readers: those who have the knowledge of the Jewish tradition would have associations with the "sacred cows" which the author ridicules.

Another mystical theme used in American Jewish fiction is reincarnation. Nathan Englander calls his short story "The Gilgul of Park Avenue" (Gilgul means reincarnation in Hebrew, which is never translated but explained later on in the story). The story starts with the beginning of the Jewish day – when the three stars are visible in the sky and the main character named Charles Morton Luger all of a sudden realizes in a taxi that he is a bearer of a Jewish soul.

He thinks of it as a rebirth and looks at the world through Jewish eyes.

The trouble starts when half an hour later at home he cannot eat a creamed chicken. "When they sat down to dinner Charles stared at his plate. Half an hour Jewish and already he felt obliged. He knew there were dietary laws..." (Englander, 111). Charles tries to find a rabbi who would help him instead of his secular Jewish therapist. When he starts keeping kosher his wife is furious with him and calls him extreme. He thinks this is an unjust accusation. "Extreme,"

Charles felt, was too extreme a word considering all there was to know and all the laws he had yet to implement. He hadn't been to synagogue. He hadn't yet observed the Sabbath. He had only changed his diet and said a few prayers" (Englander, 122). Here Judaism is connected to the laws of *kashrut*, which the protagonist starts keeping as the first step. Charles steals a mezuzah from his neighbor's door because – as he explains to his wife, "they don't use it. Steve Fraiman had me in to see their Christmas tree last year. Their daughter is dating a black man"(127). Fraiman means "free man" in Yiddish. He is freed from his Judaism by being completely assimilated, he "doesn't use" his mezuzah, does not relate to his Jewishness. In an attempt to restore her husband's sanity, his wife invites his analyst for a kosher paper plate dinner. The psychoanalysis is seen as one of contemporary forms of idol worship. It substitutes the religious belief but also plays the role of "opium for the people". The analyst is a secular Jew, Dr. Birnbaum. He claims to be Charles's spiritual adviser. He tries to convince the Rabbi to join him to help the situation. The Rabbi suggests that Dr. Birnbaum give Charles his blessing. These expressions hint to a analyst's role as a secular priest.

The Rabbi who came to support Charles tells the analyst:" ... They don't control. They absolve. Like atheist priests. No responsibility for your actions, no one to answer to. Anarchists with advanced degrees...You can't give people permission to ignore God. It is not your right" (132).
When the Rabbi blesses the bread Dr. Birnbaum reluctantly mutters "amen" which is the traditional response to a blessing. Dr. Birnbaum's own Judaism is "suppressed" by his civilized Americanness and his Jewish education is "sublimated"' into a secular education. He has a profession any Jewish mother can be proud of. The transformation from a Christian nonbeliever to an Orthodox Jew is grotesque, but all Charles wants is to be loved by his wife as he is: "He struggled to stand without judgement... to ne wholly seen, wanting her to love him changed." (137). But both Charles's wife and Dr. Birnbaum are ready to accept anything but this metamorphosis. Dr. Birnbaum asks: "Are you sure it might not be something else – like gardening or meditation? Have you considered philanthropy...as a for-instance?" (133). His wife is even ready to put up with an affair:"I've been waiting for your midlife crisis. But I expected something I could handle, a small test...Something to rise above and prove my

love for you in a grand display of resilience. Why couldn't you have turned into a vegan? Or a liberal Democrat? Slept with your secretary for real"(122).

Adam Meyer thinks that Charles Luger's transformation can be read as allegorical representation of Jewish American fiction. In his WASP incarnation Charles represents second-generation Jewish American writers who moved away from Judaism. The Jewish Charles represents the third-generation writers who want to make Judaism a focal part of their life and writings. They are determined not to compromise themselves to gain approval of the broader society, expecting their audiences to accept them as they are (116-17).

I would rather read it as a parable of a multiple identity problem in contemporary society, where one person can have more than one identity in one lifetime. Even if the change is extreme, strange and difficult to accept – the rituals are different, but what is important always stays the same. "No different as before. Different rituals, maybe. Different foods. But the same man. Only that I feel peaceful, fulfilled" (Englander, 133). The story represents people who abruptly change their way of life and risk losing their loved ones. Often keeping the rituals is more important than hurting other people's feelings. A person who is in search for his identity often faces incomprehension. But there is hope that people can learn to accept each other in different reincarnations, even if the change is much more drastic than just a new hobby. It is a call for tolerance, patience and understanding.

3. Place

Judaism is connected to the biblical Land of Israel because, according to the Bible, it was promised by God to the Jewish people. The longing for Zion is reflected in centuries of liturgical and rabbinical works.

Diaspora is another unique feature of the Jewish history. Jews had fled the persecutions and dispersed to different parts of the world, where they had been living for centuries. Thus, Jewish history is connected to different places with Israel being the biblical homeland.

Location as a spiritual and physical place is a part of identity, it plays an important role in immigrant literature. Jewish American literature is no exception. Identities shift with changing places and bridges are built between the Old and the New world.

More than one half of Mary Antin's novel is set in the Old World, in her home town in the Russian Empire. The first part of Abraham Cahan's The Rise of David Levinsky is also set in the old country. There is a big contrast between the past and the future, the Old and the New world.

Contemporary writers have novels or parts of novels set in Europe or Israel. Some characters go to Israel to search for their ancestry, some go searching for the less remote past to the shtetl in Eastern Europe. In immigrant novels characters' movement was from Eastern Europe to America. In the novels written by their grandchildren the movement is in the opposite direction, going back in space and time.

3.1 The Lower East Side

It would be incomplete to write about Jewish American experience without mentioning the Lower East Side. According to Hasja Diner, it became the epicenter of American Jewish memory and assumed a sacred status in the consciousness of American Jews (Lower East Side, 19). It is also inseparable from the general American history, because it was influenced and shaped by immigrant culture. This is where Jewish and American cultures merged and influenced each other on different levels. It represents a whole era and a certain type of life, which its name evokes. "The name "Lower East Side" contains meaning that is automatically understood by all as distinctive, replete with a set of icons associated with it…" (Diner, Lower East Side, 31).

By the beginning of the twentieth century, the Lower East Side became the center of the Jewish population. According to Rischin, by 1900 immigrants constituted over 76 % of the city's population (9). It was the time of the mass exodus of Jews from Eastern Europe. One third of the Jewish population tried to escape poverty and pogroms coming to America.

At this time the Lower East Side was an exotic place, which was closed to strangers. Its inhabitants were sealed off from the rest of American world. Although it is known that not only the Jews lived there, it was "a sprawling zone where pockets of Jewish life functioned alongside areas shaped by other peoples, many of whom were also newcomers to America," the Lower East Side came to represent the Jewish immigrant history (Diner, Lower East Side, 44). "No other ethnic group in America, with the exception of the African-American construction of Harlem, has so thoroughly understood, imagined and represented itself through a particular chunk of space" (Lower East Side, 50). In Abraham Cahan's novel, the "I Discover America" section of the book plays in the heart of the Jewish East Side. "The place... shaped David Levinsky's life and Cahan's narrative" (Lower East Side, 71). The location is used to make fictional events look authentic.

In the eyes of an outsider it is a horrible, scary place packed with people. Such an outsider is Henry James, who describes the Lower East Side in The American Scene. In New York the observer is surrounded by "alienism unmistakable...undisguised and unashamed" (James, 89). The fact that immigrants feel at home in America already after a short time makes him feel strange. He describes the Ghetto in negative terms like "the sense... of a great swarming" (93), "Jewry that burst all bounds", "ant-like population" (94). He is filled with a sense of disgust. Jews are compared to fish of over-developed proboscis, snakes and worms – anything but human beings. The many children are not a source of joy – this is "multiplication with a vengeance" (94), a sign of "Hebrew conquest of New York" (95). He cannot help but notice the modernizing of "The New Jerusalem," as he calls it. There are things like the machinery for producing electricity, fire escapes and phone lines. He notices that there is development in the poorest neighborhood, but for him it is nothing but "...organized cage for the nimbler class of animals in some great zoological garden... for human squirrels and monkeys" (96). Presence of Jewish shops and the fact that they cater to the needs of immigrants and are "taken for granted" is a bad omen – the immigrants are successfully appropriating the territory. A public garden which provides for the recreation of the newly arrived immigrants speaks for him of "Jerusalem disinfected" (96). Presence of a school is a sign of the uplifting influence America has on the swarming ordes of dirty immigrants. He gives all Jews one "insistent, defiant, unhumorous, exotic" face, calling them all by a generic name "Jerusalem" (97).

It reminds of how the Nazis gave to all Jews common middle names like Israel and Sara, thus depriving them of individuality. The word "disinfected" could not have been associated by James with concentration camps, but it completes the dehumanizing picture he is presenting. This alien, sordid, squalid and gross presence defies him and takes "his" America away by inhabiting and appropriating New York City and the English language.

Abraham Cahan describes the Lower East Side from the point of view of an insider. One of his goals is to reach an "outside" Gentile reader and to make the inhabitants of the Lower East Side human in their eyes.

For David Levinsky, it is the first place in America he sets foot in -- the gateway to his new homeland. The choice of place in this book is not accidental, because as an immigrant, the chances were high that Levinsky would settle on the Lower East Side. For him, it is not a place full of abject poverty and despair, but the first glimpse of America. He sees it in a different light than James. It is a big improvement over the *Shtetl* life. People are better dressed than in his home town. On his first day he takes a walk in the Ghetto and sees a family who are evicted from their home sitting on the sidewalk, their belongings and furniture clustered near them. The furniture of this evicted family would be a sign of prosperity in his native Antomir. The signs of poverty are inverted into a promise of a better future. The first thing for David to do is to look for hospitality in the House of God. But Jewish life in America is not the same as in the Old World and the old and new ways are constantly compared. "The Beth ha Midrash was no longer the same. This house of prayer and study, literary and dramatic center, home of musical worship, office of mutual aid and brotherly communal devotion, gradually was bereft of its attractions" (Rischin, 146).

At the end of the book, Levinsky celebrates twenty five years of his arrival to America in Waldorf Astoria. His business moves to a Fifth-Avenue location, which signifies his success. But his distance from the collective fate shared by Lower East Side dwellers does not make him happier. He comes back to the Ghetto to look for his former, happier self. The figure of David Levinsky might be controversial, but it does not stand for an Anti-Semitic caricature and it shows a Jewish immigrant as a deep character with his story of suffering and success. There is a huge contrast between James's and Cahan's representation of the same place. For James, it is a scary, threatening circus bristling with aliens, whereas for Cahan, this place is important to justify the immigrants in the eyes of America in showing their humanity and struggle to assimilate.

Even today, when there are hardly any Jews left on the Lower East Side, it still remains a Jewish cultural island in the multiethnic ocean of New York City. As Laurie Gwen Shapiro writes in her essay:" ... I say with the harsh guttural G of a forth-generation Lower East Side Jew, which I am. My Jewish observance may be lacking elsewhere, but like an Israeli, the place of my birth renders me automatically Jewish, regardless of how much or how little I follow the rules" (220). Here the Lower East Side is compared to Israel in its significance as a "Jewish place" and its inhabitants have features like accent, which makes them different from others and recognizable as belonging to a certain group. For Shapiro, it is the location and not the observance of religious commandments which makes her Jewish.

3.2. Israel

Since its creation, the State Israel has become the center of contemporary Jewish identity for Jews all over the world.

For American Jews who had found a refuge and a safe haven on American soil, Israel in a way plays a role of a "rival" for loyalty. This duality of allegiance causes characters to make difficult choices.

Israel is connected with the Hebrew culture, socialist and Zionist movements, the ideal of a "New Jew," the strong and masculine superman.

In certain aspects, this culture stands in opposition to American mostly Ashkenazic Yiddish culture.

Tova Reich expresses the importance of place for the Jewish people and all monotheist religions:

> ...Old City of Jerusalem, achingly close to Mount Moriah, upon whose pinnacle Abraham raised the gleaming slaughter knife over the tender throat of his son Isaac. Upon the black rock that Jews call *even hashettiya,* stone of the foundation, and Christians *omphalos mundi,* *t*he bellybutton of the world, Abraham bound the hald-brother of his eldest son, Ishmael. From this black rock the prophet Mohammed was launched into heaven, leaving behind his most delicate footprint, and over it, to honor this passage, his followers erected the sparkling golden dome. This black rock, perhaps the site

of the priestly offering in the Holiest of Holies, is certainly the absolute center of the earth; dislodge it, and all of creation would be sucked into the hole, like a whirlpool down the drain, back into chaos and void and nothingness. (The Master of Return 126-127)

Andrew Furman classifies different time periods by their relationship to Israel as pre-Zionist, Zionist and Post-Zionist.

The pre-Zionist period is from the time of Theodor's Herzl's first Zionist Congress in 1897 in Basel until roughly 1947, when Zionism was unpopular among the American Jews. Zionist period begins with the miraculous founding of the State of Israel in 1948 and reaches zenith in 1967 during the Six-Day War. The Post-Zionist period begins in 1990's when the critical approach among the liberal circles lead to divided opinions and to questioning Israeli political actions (Furman, Imagination, 6).

For a long time, there was no doubt that being Jewish meant living in the Land of Israel and the Diaspora existence was only temporary now, that the Jewish homeland was restored and there was a place to go back.

The United States is compared to Israel in many works of fiction. There is a kind of a "competition" between the promised lands – America, "the *goldene medine*" -- a golden land of a private pursuit of happiness, and Israel, the land of fathers promised to the Jewish people in the Torah, where one's private interests sometimes clash with the interests of a group, a state or a nation.

Tova Reich underscores the stereotypes of America's vices versus Israel's glory in Jewish War, where a character's life story is changed by reading Leon Uris:

> Elkanan Ben-Canaan...was a compact, muscular, intense man, from Galveston, Texas, originally, Eddie Cohen he had been called in those days, whose life had been changed irrevocably when he picked up the novel Exodus in an airport lounge before boarding his flight from Houston to Los Angeles, where he was journeying in the hope of launching a career as a movie stunt man. Within a month, he was on his way across the American continent corrupted by its cowboys and its commercials, across the ocean polluted by its sunken luxury liners and pirate ships, across the decadence and gas chambers of Europe – to Israel. (Jewish War, 113)

In Philip Roth's Counterlife, location in general, and Israel in particular play central roles in the book. In the second chapter called "Judea," his narrator and alter ego Nathan Zuckermann, in his discussions with other characters expresses the sentiments of many Jews in America or elsewhere have or feel about Israel.

When his friend's father shows him the view of Jerusalem out of a window he says: "See that tree?..That's a Jewish tree. See that bird? It's a Jewish bird. See, up there? A Jewish cloud. There is no country for a Jew but here" (Roth, 52).

The argument which follows seems to express inner voice of many secular American Jews who feel at home in New Jersey, in Chicago, or elsewhere, and who don't have strong religious attachment to the historical homeland, as Israel is called in Jewish rhetoric. It is about definition of homeland and identity.

> My landscape wasn't the Negev wilderness, or the galilean hills, or the coastal plain of ancient Philistia; it was industrial, immigrant America - Newark where I'd been raised, Chicago where I'd been educated, and New York where I was living in a basement apartment on a Lower East Side street among poor Ukrainians and Puerto Ricans. My sacred text wasn't the Bible but novels translated from Russian, German, and French into the language which I was beginning to write and publish my own fiction - not the semantic range of classical Hebrew but the jumpy beat of American English was what excited me. (Roth, 53)

Zuckerman's New York apartment is on the Lower East Side – the ultimate Jewish place in America, but the Jewish inhabitants had long moved to their American-dream houses in the suburbs. His neighbors are Ukrainians and Puerto Ricans, who have inherited the immigrant space.

The brand of Zionism of his grandfather who "reached the same prophetic conclusion as Theodor Herzl -- that there was no future for them in Christian Europe", was "to save their own Jewish skins" (53). They had wanted to survive as Jews, but instead of going to Palestine to rebuild the Jewish state, they set off to America for their individual pursuit of freedom from persecution and their individual happiness.

Here the difference between the two "promised lands" is most apparent -- America is supposed not to differentiate between Jews or Gentiles, the American dream is there for everyone, as Zuckerman puts it: "...I could not think of any historical society that had achieved the level of tolerance institutionalized in America or that had placed pluralism smack at the center of its publicly advertised dream of itself" (Roth, 54). He is a patriot of America as much as his Israeli peer Shuki is a patriot of Israel. Can he be American and Jewish at the same time? Or is the Jewish part unimportant – after all Zuckermann has four

Gentile wives and does not think much of circumcising his unborn son, until faced with virulent Anti-Semitism. Or does the American part have to disappear, as is the case of his brother Henry, who goes to live in a settlement in Judea to find himself as a Jew in a community of English speakers, most of whom are American born?

Zuckerman's brother changes his name to Hanoch and decides to reject his past American life. His individuality is now minor compared to group interests. "*Me* is somebody *I* have forgotten. *Me* no longer exist out here. There isn't a time for *me*, there isn't need for *me* – here Judea counts, not *me!*" (105). Individual interests against group allegiance is ostensibly what constitutes the major difference between the American and Israeli Jews, "Hanoch of Judea against Henry of Jersey." For Zuckerman's father "militant, triumphant Israel was...their avenger for the centuries and centuries of humiliating oppression; the state created by Jews in the aftermath of the Holocaust had become for them the belated answer to the Holocaust, not only the embodiment of intrepid Jewish strength but instrument of justifiable wrath and swift reprisal" (Roth, 56). Zuckerman's father died before he could witness Menachem Begin, "who could pass, from his appearance, for the owner of a downtown clothing store." This would make his father so proud: "After all, who better than the Jew ridiculed and despised for his funny accent and his ugly looks and his alien ways, to make it perfectly clear to everyone that what matters now isn't what goyim think but what Jews do?" (Roth, 57).

The question is not which one of the two homelands is better, but which one is the true homeland. After the former immigrants reached their goal of achieving positions in society and acquiring wealth, their grandchildren are coming to realize that something is missing. "In America there are young religious people, even secular people..., who are tired of purposeless living. Here in Judea there is a purpose and meaning, so they come" (Roth, 124). In this comparison between the United States and Israel, Israel itself is not homogeneous. It consists of two parts, the secular and the religious. The city of Tel Aviv represents the secular Israel, which wants to be "normal," just like every other nation on one side and religious Jerusalem and Hebron on another. "This is where the Jews began, not in Tel Aviv but here" (Roth, 109).

Natan Englander's short story "In This Way We Are Wise" takes place in

Jerusalem, in a familiar neighborhood where the author/narrator has just witnessed a terror attack. The location is marked by recent tragic events: "Every spot where a corpse lay is marked by candles" (203). The Israel of an American is different from real Israel. It is an imaginary place, like a theater where great historical events are staged. It is a moving picture, a sacred place seen from afar:

> A biblical Israel, crowded with warriors and prophets, fallen kings and common men conscripted to do God's will. An American boy's Israel. A child raised up on causality and symbol.
> Holocaust as wrath of God. Israel the Phoenix rising up from the ashes.
> I was raised on tradition...A Jerusalem so precious God spared it when He flooded the world...I thought I learned everything about Jerusalem, only to discover my information was very very old. (199, 203)

Jerusalem after a terrorist attack is a controversial place to (re)find God.

> Today is a day to find religion. To decide that one god is more right than another, to uncover in this sad reality a covenant – some promise of coming good...If one is willing to turn again to his old knowing, to salt over shoulders, prayers before journeys, wrists bound with holy red thread. Witchery and superstition. Comforts. (204)

Religious faith is seen as remedy for the uncertain existence in modern world plagued by wars and terror.

Many modern writers use Israel's absence from the map as an important part of the narrative. They try to imagine what the world in general and the Jewish world in particular would be like if Israel weren't there.

In Marge Piercy's He She and It, Israel is annihilated by the terrorists, it is a nuclear wasteland where nothing can survive. The annihilation story is told in the first pages of the book so that the reader is faced with the horrific reality of this utopia. The main character's husband Josh is a child of Israeli parents, "survivors of the Two Week War a terrorist had launched with a nuclear device that had burned Jerusalem off the map, a conflagration of biological, chemical and nuclear weapons that had set the oil-fields aflame and destroyed the entire region" (Piercy, 3). After this incident, the world blames the Jews for all disasters and many are killed by fellow citizens. "...Jew-hunting mobs, burning houses...nasty stuff that followed the Two Week War" (384). Josh's parents are "killed in fighting in the Jewish quarter of Munich, to which many Russian Jews and ex-Israelis had fled" (391). That is how the town of Tikva, (Hebrew for hope and also the name of Israeli national anthem), was founded. What is left of Israel is called "a Black Zone" because it is black on the map, radioactive and supposedly unpopulated. Later in the novel we meet Shira's mother's companion Nili, who is recognizable by her accent, identified by Shira as

> of someone who has grown up speaking Hebrew...It was mostly older people who did, from when there had been an Israel, from before the Two Week War, from before the interdiction that quarantined the entire bombed out, radioactive, biologically unsafe area that had been Israel, Jordan, Lebanon, Syria, Iraq and a good hunk of Saudi Arabia. (Piercy, 188)

It turns out that Nili is a woman warrior from Safed, Israel, a place which has a very special status in the history of Kabbala, the Jewish mysticism. The creation of Golem is connected with the lore of Kabbala. Nili is a member of community of descendants of Israeli and Palestinian women who survived the nuclear annihilation. It is a matriarchal society, where there are no men. To procreate, they clone and engineer genes and undergo additional alteration after birth. In a way they are their own golems: self-created saviours and protectors.

They believe in education – something that was the privilege of male scholars in the Jewish tradition. Nili claims: "We are people of the book. We have always considered getting knowledge part of being human... We have created ourselves to endure, to survive, to hold our land. Soon we will begin rebuilding Yerushalaim"(194, 198). She compares herself to the dove or a raven from Noah's ark, who flies to see if the world is safe to go out.

In the end of the novel, the grandmother Malka is going to Israel with Nili to have her eyesight restored. She is excited about meeting Nili's people, "the strongest women in the world" (417). Israel symbolizes rebirth, it is the final destination, the setting for messianic aspirations, restoration, renewal and hope, a metaphor for eternal youth. All other places are temporary havens, even the town of Tikva. It is the women of Israel who represent hope, and who are going to restore *Yerushalaim*. The Messiah, who in the Jewish tradition has to come and restore Jerusalem is male, but here the tradition is kept up only by women scholars living in Safed, the city of (male) scholars of Kabbala. The tradition is adjusted to a feminist vision of the future and connected to Israel as a place of hope for renewal.

There is a parallel in Malka's *aliya* (ascent to Israel) to the *aliya* of Maharal's granddaughter Chava from the parallel story about the Golem of Prague, which Malka tells Yod the cyborg. Chava's dream never comes true – she dies in the middle of her journey in Sofia of food poisoning. Her death symbolizes the aspirations of generations of Jewish women which never came true. Malka says: "As Chava went, so I go, casting myself on the wind in hope, traveling toward the hidden light I pray soon be shining into me, a fountain of light in which I can plunge myself" (419). The ability to see symbolizes hope and restoration, which are connected to Israel, where Malka's eyes will be operated on by female doctors.

Malka also has a similarity to Piercy's own grandmother who was a great storyteller. "Her best stories came from the rich pack of folklore of the women of the shtetl, a world of brutal violence and powerful magic."

(Sleeping with Cats, 34). The story of the golem Piercy used in He, She and It came from her grandmother.

Another Israeli woman character is Carmela Yovel in Tova Reich's Jewish War. She embodies a masculine woman, an almost comic book Israeli stereotype: "At'halta D'Geula's mother, Carmela Yovel, was an Israeli, born on a kibbutz, a major in the army, a trained markswoman and a sharpshooter..." (71).

Israel is an opposite of Diaspora where a new type of a warrior Jew is born. It is a country where women serve in the army, the Israeli Defence Force, and carry guns just like men. Here an Israeli female character represents the new type of a Jew who is not afraid of anything. She makes her husband sign the divorce papers at a gun point. In Israel, all weddings and divorces go through the Orthodox rabbinical court and it is only men who can write a divorce letter. Carmela takes her fate in her own hands. She flies off to the United States to make her fortune with a pistol and a toothbrush in her pocket. Since her business was not quite legal she takes "advantage of the Law of Return and of the honorable idealistic refusal of the State to extradite and Jew wanted for an alleged crime allegedly perpetrated in the diaspora – for the tragic fate of Jews in alien courtrooms and foreign prison cells is well documented" (Jewish War, 73).

In the parallel world of Michael Chabon's Yiddish Policemen Union, just like in Marge Piercy's utopia, Israel is annihilated at the moment of its birth in

1948 and the Jews were thrown into the sea. America gives temporary refuge to the European Jews who escape the Holocaust and allows them to settle in Alaska, but they never get the American rights and citizenship. This is the "Yiddishland" called Sitka, where Yiddish is the official language, the Jews are cheerfully called "the frozen chosen" and the US American Jews are called "Mexicans."

The reality of this "parallel universe" is grim and hopeless.

> The Holy Land has never seemed more remote or unattainable than it does to a Jew of Sitka...For half a century, Arab strongmen and Muslim partisans, Persians and Egyptians...pan-Arabists and pan-Islamists, traditionalists and the Party of Ali, have all sunk their teeth into Eretz Yisroel and worried it down to bone and gristle. Jerusalem is a city of blood and slogans painted on the wall, severed heads on telephone poles. (Chabon, 17)

The Land of Israel – *Eretz Yisroel* is phonetically transcribed in Yiddish, not in Hebrew, like it is common to pronounce it today. The story is told in a few succinct horrifying phrases: "Nineteen forty-eight: Strange times to be a Jew. In August the defence of Jerusalem collapsed and the outnumbered Jews of the three-month-old republic of Israel were routed, massacred, and driven into the sea" (29). The situation of the Jews is very difficult, their refuge only temporary. They soon have to leave Sitka because the territory goes back under "Reversion." The plot turns around a messianic figure of the Chassidic Rabbi's son, Mendel Shpilman, who has been murdered. He used to cure the sick with his blessings, but fled his home before his arranged wedding. The stories of miracles he worked go around. He is supposed to be "the Righteous man of the Generation" who is a potential Messiah.

Mendel is also the name of the late Rebbe of Lubavich, who was an influential figure in the Jewish world and was believed to be the Messiah by members of Chabad Lubavich movement. Mendel's father explains: "We are taught by the Baal Shem Tov, of blessed memory, that a man with the potential to be Messiah is born into every generation. This is the Tzaddik Ha-Dor" (Chabon, 141). Baal Shem Tov was the founder of the Chassidic movement who lived in the seventeenth century.

Detective Landsman investigates Mendel's murder. Before his death he was known to be a gay heroin addict. Bina, Landsman's ex-wife, recites a verse from

Isaiah 53:3: "He is despised and rejected of men...a man of sorrows and acquainted with grief" (169).

Detective Landsmann finds out about a conspiracy to return to Israel in order to build the Third Temple. For that a red heifer is raised on a secret farm.

> When the Temple of Jerusalem is restored...and it's time to make the traditional sin offering, the Bible says you need a particualr kind of a cow. A red heifer, without blemish. Pure...I believe there have been only nine of them since the beginning of history. (295)
> Then you kill it...And you burn it to ashes, and you make a paste of the ashes, and you dab a little of that on your priests. Otherwise they can't go unto the Sanctuary...because they are unclean... (315)

The only problem is, the Dome of the Rock is still standing on the precise cite of the Temple. "The spot where Abraham went to sacrifice Isaak, where Jacob saw the ladder reaching up to heaven" (315).

It turns out that the American Christian government stands behind the plot to blow up the mosque. They are interested to get the holy Land back to the Jews because they believe *their* Messiah is coming back when it's done.

The Verbover Rebbe whose son was the potential messiah says, "I pity the gentiles for their childlike trust in the imminent return of one who never in the first place departed, let alone arrived. But I am quite sure that they, in turn, pity us our own tardy Messiah" (Chabon, 343).

The plan to blow up the Dome of the Rock is carried out even though the potential messiah is murdered. The messianic aspirations for the redemption of the World are connected to the Holy Land. But Detective Landsman is happy in the Diaspora, his home is where he is happy. A home of the Jewish people is set against a home of an individual Jew. The individual pursuit of happiness does not go along with the salvation of the world.

> ...there is no Messiah of Sitka. Landsman has no home, no future, no fate but Bina. The land that he and she were promised was bounded only by the fringes of their wedding canopy, by the dog-eared corners of their cards of membership in an international fraternity whose members carry their patrimony in a tote bag, their world on the tip of the tongue. (Chabon, 411)

Tova Reich's The Jewish War is set both in America and Israel. The movement from land to land is a reverse from early immigrant novels, where the characters came to their final destination, the Promised Land of America from the Old World. Here they go to the Promised Land of Israel from America.

The novel begins in Machpelah in Hebron where the forefathers and foremothers of the Jewish people are buried. The Kingdom of Judea and Samaria is announced and its King is Yehudi HaGoel (saviour in Hebrew). His first official act is to "announce formally ... secession from the State of Israel" (Reich, 5). Then there is a flashback to the time when the two main characters Yehudi and Hoshea come to Israel during the Six Day War in coffins, since all air traffic to the Middle East is closed because of the war. They remove the corpses of two deceased Holocaust survivors – this desecration of Holocaust victims is the price they have to pay for getting to Israel. The metaphor of rebirth as it is attached to place alludes to immigrant's change of life and goes back to Mary Antin.

> Enclosed within the coffin, it seemed to Yehudi that he had been bracketed out of time. He was in a holding stage, as in a cocoon. It was as if he had died in America and would be resurrected in Israel, with the help of God, in the old Jewish graveyard in Hebron, as specified on the ticket. Between this death and this rebirth he was, as he saw it, condemned to endure a period of extreme turmoil and turbulence inside the coffin, in a state of utter passivity and helplessness... (52).

American Jews were indoctrinated with Israel as the cornerstone of their Jewish identity. Herbie – Hoshea organized a program at a Jewish summer resort, where he would talk about the great modern-day State of Israel:

> And then he would seize and wring their hearts like dishrags, purge the dross from their souls with an account of the modern-day State of Israel – draining the swamps, reclaiming the deserts, campfires and accordions and *horas,* stunned dark-skinned girl soldiers in tight khaki uniforms, boy soldiers with knitted yarmulkes clipped to their hair leaning on submachine guns, an open Talmud spread out in front of them across the back of a tank. Ah, Jerusalem...her cupolas golden in the sunset...the novelty, the glorious novelty, of healthy Jews with muscles and good teeth, nerve and sass.
> By the end of the evening Hoshea had them all on their feet belting out the *Hatikva,* chills running audibly up and down their spines... (Reich, 18)

This is a deliberately stereotypical representation of Israel like a one-dimensional romantic picture. The heroic Israelis did all the hard work so that American Jews can tell patriotic stories about them. The boys are warriors and scholars, as in ancient pre-Diaspora days, and the girls soldiers are sexualized by their "tight uniforms." This idealistic picture is represented to raise as much money as possible from people, most of whom would never leave their comfortable lives in order to move to Israel.

Israel represents the new kind of Jew who is not afraid of pogroms and Antisemitism anymore, a Jew who tills the land, works physically, who is a scholar and a warrior at the same time and speaks the revived modern Hebrew. This is an ideal Jew, a role model for Diaspora Jews. But Reich presents to the reader an ironic, post-Zionist picture.

Hoshea's fiancee Faith Fleishmann who afterwards becomes Emuna (meaning Faith in Hebrew) suddenly decides to postpone their wedding and instead of going to Israel decides to join the Peace Corps. The reason is she wants to get away from her Jewishness.

> She was tired, Faith said, to drag her Jewishness around on her back every single minute as her only legitimate reference point...Her Jewishness was only one aspect of her identity; she was more than just Jewish...Like what else was she, for example? Like a woman...Certainly, Hoshea agreed, a Jewish woman...
> She wanted to get away, to become an American. Israel wasn't really getting away; Israel was just another Jewish neighborhood, like Flatbush or Brighton Beach or Borough Park. (44-45)

In Faith's geography Israel is a part of Jewish America, she wants to taste something really new. She would like "to have fun" and get away from Jewish geography. Hoshea's reaction is that

> ...given her backgrounds and upbringing, she wouldn't even be able to recognize fun if it hit her over the head and waltzed her around the planet...Who ever heard of plunging voluntarily into the mud and dirt and poverty and disease of one of those Peace Corps villages as a way of having fun? Only a masochistic, guilt-stricken Jew would think of that. Why did she believe that the grass was...more rotten in the other guy's backyard? Besides, since when was the pursuit of happiness number one on the Jewish hit parade? If I forget thee, O Jerusalem, let my right hand forget its cunning, let my tongue cleave to the roof of my mouth if I remember thee not, if I do not place Jerusalem *above all my happiness*...she wanted to be happy...to be light and airy like an American, like a gentile, instead of Jewish...always gloomy, anticipating calamity any minute..." (46)

Psalm 137:1-6 is called to mind, where the Babylonian exiles cry by the rivers of Babylon, remembering Zion.

Jerusalem should be placed above the individual pursuit of happiness, which in this case means going to Africa for two years to "have fun" as a Peace Corps worker. Ironically, she is accused of selfishness because she wants to do the most selfless thing – commit a few years of her life to helping people in poor countries. The Jewish idea of *Tikkun Olam*, repairing the world, is Faith's point of reference, but she does not recognize it. She wants to get away from being Jewish by helping others only to remain in the tradition, which places great importance on social engagement and helping others.

Hoshea dreams of *aliya* – ascent to the Land of Israel. The audience at the resort donates money for his aliya fund. He is supposed to make aliya for all of them. This is compared to the old custom of Kapara chicken on Yom Kippur, the Day of Atonement. It is an ancient custom which symbolically expresses recognition that one has sinned and is no longer deserving of life.

The *Kaparot* ritual involves taking a chicken in the right hand and revolving it over the head while reciting a prayer. The chicken is then slaughtered and is given to the poor. Today, most people use money instead of chicken, the money goes to charity. Hoshea would be sent to Israel instead of the American Jews who give him money, like the "fowl of atonement." He is a ritual sacrifice for the others who are too afraid or too comfortable to make aliya themselves. It is a bitter satire on Zionism of American Jews, who were willing to donate money for the cause, but rarely willing to make aliya themselves.

But not all of them are like this. Yehudi HaGoel's wife, Michelle (Shelly) Kugel is the only daughter of a rich man, who goes to Barnard College. She follows her husband to Israel, bears him eleven children and puts up with his taking another two wives. She protests when he takes the second wife, but herself suggests that he take the third wife, so that life becomes easier for her. The most poignant moment characterizing her new life is when the settlers gather in the settlement of Yamit to protest Israel's giving back of Sinai to Egypt.

> The women, chained together in pairs, resisted like lionesses, shrieking,...ten soldiers were required to subdue Carmela, dragging Shelly like dead weight behind her. ... So ferocious was Carmela in her resistance, that while the other women were loaded a dozen to a cage, Carmela was stuffed into a separate cage, with Shelly, heavy and inert, attached. As their private cage was lifted high up into the air by the helicopter, Shelly sighed. "At last," she said, summoning up, in this wilderness, her Ivy League education, "a room of one's own." Then she noticed Carmela, howling at her side. "Well, almost," she amended, "almost, but not quite. Still, it's probably the best I can expect under the circumstances." (Reich, 119)

The tragic incongruence of the situation, being evacuated by the police, the terrible attack, the cage contrast the "Ivy League" thoughts of personal individual comfort. Here, in a place where life is sacrificed for the sake of a group ideal, dreaming of a room of one's own sounds like a grotesque joke.

3. 3. Europe

Europe is a place where Jews had lived for centuries and where they had been persecuted and murdered.

In many contemporary works of American Jewish fiction, Europe is a place which characters visit to rediscover their roots and heritage, a place which triggers memories connected to events in history.

In Roth's Counterlife the main character Zuckerman comes to live in England with his English wife. When he encounters Antisemitism, which is embedded in European culture, at first he is shocked, then it triggers his reaction in becoming "more Jewish than ever." The comparison with America is very meaningful – there

Antisemitism is marginal, here in England it is a part of culture.

Zuckerman discovers that his aristocratic mother-in-law and sister-in-law are virulent Antisemites. Roth re-creates the experience of many second-generation American Jews who had never experienced European Antisemitism firsthand, but learned of it from their family tradition.

During the final argument before the break-up of their relationship, Zuckerman's wife flings at him: "Go back to America, please, where everybody loves Jews – you think!" (Roth, 306).

Zuckerman is shocked by his reaction and is trying to explain it to himself:

> the unpredictable development was how furious it all made me...my writing had hardly been born of recklessness or naivete about the Jewish history of pain; I had written my fiction in the knowledge of it...the fact remained that...the experience of it had been negligible in my personal life. Crossing back to Christian Europe nearly a hundred years after my grandparents' westward escape, I was finally feeling up against my skin that outer reality which I'd mostly come to know in America as an "abnormal" inner preoccupation permeating nearly everything with the Jewish world. (Roth, 307)

Zuckerman explains why he wants to circumcise his son, who, according to the Jewish Orthodox tradition, would not be Jewish because his mother isn't. He points out the importance of humanitarian values of Judaism: "The heavy hand of human values falls upon you right at the start, marking your genitals as its own" (Counterlife, 323). In Israel he told his friend that this is only an unimportant ritual, but he changes his opinion in England: "I find myself in a situation that has reactivated the strong sense of difference that had all but atrophied in New York...Circumcision confirms that there is an us, and an us that isn't solely him and me. England 's made a Jew of me in only eight weeks, which, on reflection, might be the least painful method" (324). Going to England made Zuckerman re-evaluate his relation to his ethnicity, becomes "more Jewish than ever" out of protest, as a reaction to Antisemitism, which is he had not experienced in America on the same scale.

3.3.1 Ukraine

Eastern Europe is a setting for centuries of Jewish history.

The biggest wave of Jewish immigration came to the United States from Eastern Europe in the time between 1880's up to 1924.

One of the countries which had a very big Jewish population was Ukraine, a land with tragic history for the Jewish people. It is associated with pogroms, Bogdan Chmelnyzkyj massacre and a long tradition of Antisemitism. Ukraine becomes an important setting for contemporary American Jewish authors.

In Jewish War Tova Reich uses the stereotype of Antisemitic Ukrainians. There is a battle of almost biblical proportions between Jewish and Ukrainian youth camps in the Catskills. Kugel's Hotel suffers harassment from Camp Chernobyl, a summer resort for Ukrainians. The camp's director and "his cohorts, a gang of professional pogromists"(35), claim that camp Chernobyl has a right to use the lake since a portion of it intrudes into their property. Hy Kugel is worried how his guests, many of whom are Holocaust survivors, would react "to the spectacle of a squad of anti-Semitic Ukrainian hoodlums in full folk regalia" (35). Moreover, the Catskills are claimed by the Jewish people and acknowledged as Jewish territory. "The Jews had planted their flag upon them...The Catskills belonged to the Jews like any other God-given birthright" (36). Disturbing incidents start happening: a rowboat which had disappeared turns up later "inscribed with a swastika and a message faulting "Adolf" for not having finished the job." (36) One day Shelly Kugel and Rabbi's daughter are abducted in a rowboat. Shelly tells the Ukrainian abductors she has "a very bad disease – Semitemia gravus...A totally incurable Jewish disease..." (37). "Chernobyl gangsters" are so scared that they vanish "clutching for protection the steel crucifixes suspended from their necks" (37).

Kugel men organise demonstrations, waving the signs that children have made in the arts and crafts workshop: "Let My Lake Go", "Remember the Six Million", "Long Live Israel." The matter is becoming serious. One day, a Ukrainian named Bogdan (evoking Bogdan Chmelnyzkyj) steps out. He has a stature of Goliath and his only passion is body-building. His heart is tattooed with a crucifix. He challenges the Jews to send their "best guy." After a few days when nobody has ventured to step forward, there appears a "little Jew." The David of the Catskills is Yehudi HaGoel – still formally known as Jerry Goldberg. He is dressed up as a doctor. He tricks the Ukrainian giant and gives him a shot out of a huge syringe. "A Jewish shot, for your own protection...just a dose of Jewish germs..." (41). Bogdan is so terrified that he collapses. The Jews are celebrating victory.

Reich shows stereotypes of Ukrainians as professional pogromists and Antisemites. The whole story is grotesque and exaggerated. Reich targets prejudices, hatred and fear on both sides.

Reich uses Ukraine also in Master of the Return. The main setting of the novel is Israel, but the main character Samuel Himmelhoch had aspired all his life to go to Uman in Ukraine to pray at the holy site to correct his evil inclinations. He never reaches it. Uman is the gravesite of a famous Chassidic Rabbi and wonder maker Rebbe Nachman of Bretslav. It is a holy site for Chassidic Jews. American Jew who went to live in Israel wants to go to Ukraine on a spiritual journey and it is as unreachable to him as Israel had been for his ancestors. He comes close a few times, even reaches the Soviet Union with his friends using false Mexican passports. But Samuel is not allowed to go to Uman along with his friends, he stays in a sealed room at the airport. Uman as a source of spirituality remains an unreachable, closed and mysterious place. But times change.

In Jonathan Foyer's Everything is Illuminated Ukraine is the place of origin connected to the Holocaust. It is a book with auto-biographical elements describing the author's trip to the post-perestroika Ukraine searching for the woman who had saved the author's grandfather from the Nazis. Since Jonathan speaks no Russian or Ukrainian he finds a translator, a young man named Alex, who speaks a peculiar version of English, which sounds like a literal translation from Russian. His father runs a travel agency, in his words: "...denominated Heritage touring. It is for Jewish people, like the hero, who have cravings to leave that ennobled country America and visit humble towns in Poland and Ukraine. Father's agency scores a translator, guide, and driver for the Jews, who try to unearth places where their families once existed" (Foer, 3). It is hard for Alex to understand that someone should be so foolish as to come from America to Ukraine, but people even pay money for it, so Alex thinks that "Jewish people were having shit between their brains" (Foer, 3).

Alex compares Ukraine and America: "Lvov is the city like New York City in America. New York City, in truth, was designed on the model of Lvov. It has very tall buildings (with as many as six levels) and comprehensive streets, (with enough room for as many as three cars) and many cellular phones" (31). Negative things are compared as well and Ukraine wins on the issue of being a dangerous place, too. Alex warns Jonathan not to leave his bags in the car because people in Ukraine take things without asking. "I have read that New York City is very dangerous, but I must say that Ukraine is more dangerous" (64).

The American explains why he came to see his grandfather's homeland: "I want to see Trachimbrod... To see what it's like, how my grandfather grew up, where I would be now if it weren't for the war." "You would be Ukrainian." "That's right." "Like me." "I guess". "Only not like me because you would be a farmer in an unimpressive town, and I live in Odessa, which is very much like Miami. "And I want to see what it's like now. I don't think there are any Jews left..." (Foer, 59).

Alex's self-esteem is restored because he lives in a counterpart town of Miami. He knows now that Jonathan might have been born a Ukrainian, so he loses some of his exotic foreign charm. But Ukraine loses its charm too, it is not a lost world one can never get too, like the unreachable Uman. The mysterious and mythological shtetl is still there, only the Jews are missing. Ukraine is not closed anymore. Grandchildren of people who were neighbors – one Ukrainian, one

Jewish, can meet and become friends. But Alex's grandfather who had betrayed his Jewish friend, Hershel, to the Germans, commits suicide. He tries to explain: "I am not a bad person... I am a good person who has lived in a bad time" (227). The horrible past still haunts daily lives in Ukraine and catches up with people who had tried to escape it.

3.3.2 Germany

In the period after the World War Two the image of Germany became connected to the darkest events in history.

Waldemar Zacharasiewicz mentions a process called the "Americanization of the Holocaust," which has strongly affected the perception of Germany in the United States. The Holocaust Museum in Washington D.C. represents a universal tragedy from a point of view of an American.

The Museum's site states:

> A living memorial to the Holocaust, the United States Holocaust Memorial Museum stimulates leaders and citizens to confront hatred, prevent genocide, promote human dignity, and strengthen democracy...the Museum provides a powerful lesson in the fragility of freedom, the myth of progress, the need for vigilance in preserving democratic values. With unique power and authenticity, the Museum teaches millions of people each year about the dangers of unchecked hatred and the need to prevent genocide.

In American Jewish literature Germany often emerges as setting for a visit to one's own former house or apartment, an attempt to find relatives.

According to Susanne Klingenstein, "the urge to visit the past – to return to one's place of origin, or to see the site of a heinous crime against one's people – is a recurring motif in recent Jewish writing" ("Visits to Germany," 7).

For many Jews – not only in America, Germany has been a forbidden territory, its language and culture being the language of the oppressors. Many of the refugees who had managed to make it to safety, were growing up with German as their mother tongue and later refused to speak it. The father of the main character Renee in Rebecca Goldstein's The Mind-Body Problem had majored in German literature and later gave up his studies, never uttering a word of German again.

Renee, who grew up religious, but has abandoned the traditional way of life, goes to Europe after having gotten married to a genius mathematician, who has no knowledge of Judaism but for his Jewish name – Noam. When they come to Vienna, he suddenly has a kind of revelation that he had already lived there. He has no prior knowledge of German but recognizes the streets, pointing at the Jewish district as his home. The Jewish tradition believes in reincarnation, but his wife does not and, as a philosophy student, thinks that all learning is recollection. Noam, for his part, strongly believes in reincarnation. "Renee, I've made the most marvelous discovery! Renee, I've been here before!...Not in this life, Renee, not in this life. Not in the life of Noam Himmel..." (Goldstein, 97). He is convinced that he had been murdered by the Nazis as a W*underkind* in Vienna in his previous life in 1938, when the Nazis invaded Vienna and the same year he was born in America. "The evidence for reincarnation is overwhelming" (99).

He also says that he was Jewish in his previous life, which makes this fact an important part of his identity. He had never realized before how important it is: "It means that my Jewishness is essential to my identity" (110). He is convinced that he has proof and accuses his wife of being blind to the truth.

Renee, who grew up in the Jewish tradition and denied it for the sake of philosophy, confronts a completely secularized husband, whose trip to Europe makes him aware of the importance of his Jewish identity. Europe makes him connect to the past through the idea of reincarnation – a continuation of one's existence as a Jew who is murdered in Europe and is reborn in the United States.

When walking through the Jewish district they enter a restaurant. Renee asks the waiter if the restaurant is kosher, he apologizingly answers that it is not, but the proprietress is Jewish. She comes to greet them, and Renee notices that the inside of her arm is stamped with the blue numbers of a concentration camp. The woman tells that she was born in Vienna right on Judenplatz, has lived in America for a few years after the war, but in the end returned to her homeland: "I am Viennese...in spite of it all. In spite of the fact that I can look out onto this square and remember when it flowed with blood. I am Viennese..." (109). This is the tragedy of the "promised land;" of high German culture which betrayed the German Jews. The idea of the "promised land" of German culture and literature was used by many assimilated Jews in Germany before the World War Two. It is mentioned in Marcel Reich-Ranizki's autobiography, where he tells how his mother described the German literature and culture as their "promised land."

When continuing their journey to Hungary, Renee stumbles upon a synagogue and a Museum which commemorates the destruction of Hungarian Jews. She follows a dwarf on a flight of stairs on a nearby street and comes to what she at first takes for a restaurant of sorts. She is told that it is a welfare kitchen where everyone is free to eat. She tells him and his companions she is an American who studies philosophy. In the end he wishes her *a guten Shabbos* – a greeting for the Sabbath that religious Jews greet each other with. She realizes she just had a traditional Shabbat meal and sees people going to the evening prayer, one of them looking like her late beloved father and it makes her miss the Shabbat meals at home. She misses the feelings she had as a child.

> ...I saw that one of them looked a little like my father: the delicate face structure, high, pronounced cheekbones, and gentle expression. I watched him disappear into the building and felt stabbed with longing...The longing in me- for my father and his world -- had risen to my eyes...suddenly I was back inside it, inside Shabbos." (Goldtsein, 123)

Visit to Europe and the site of the destruction of Jewry makes Renee go back in time to the religious environment of her home. But there is no real going back for her since she cut herself from her "previous incarnation."

As a woman and an intellectual she has rebelled against the religious tradition, which gives a woman only place and justification of existence as a wife and mother, only in order to get to a world, where getting married is her escape from a failed academic career. In the academic world, one has to look ugly and unfeminine to pursue an academic career, as her friend puts it: "feminine is dumb... it would be an act of feminist heroism... to wear eyeliner and mascara...Men don't have to make the choice, but we do. For us it's either or" (194). Renee's religious sister-in law is afraid of failure to produce offspring, in her world there is no bigger shame than being a barren woman. She thinks her miscarriages are a punishment for her sins. In the modern academic world there are fears of academic failure, of sexual failure, or loss of youth, which are no less crippling than the religious world's fears. These fears torture both women and men. When in the end of the novel Noam reveals he has lost his mathematical gift, Renee finally becomes his friend.

Philip Roth makes his protagonist Zuckerman sit on the plane from Tel Aviv to London next to a guy named Jimmy who wants to highjack the plane to Germany. He has a statement for the press once the plane lands on German soil. He demands that the Holocaust should be forgotten because it is the reason for Anti-semitism. The solution of the Jewish question according to him, is to destroy the Yad Vashem Museum and to strike the past from the memory forever.

> Israel is their prosecutor, the Jew is their judge! ... every goy in his heart is a little Eichmann. This is why the papers, at the U.N., everywhere, they all rush to make Israel the villain... This is the hatred that we keep alive by commemorating their crime at Yad Vashem...
> On German soil we abandon the Holocaust! Land in Munich and leave the nightmare where it began! Jews without a Holocaust will be Jews without enemies! Jews who are not judges will be Jews who are not judged... (Roth, 166-167).

He claims he got his ideas form the books of his idol – the author Nathan Zuckerman, whose ideal is a secularized Jew living in Christian Europe and married to a Gentile wife. This is the "final solution" of the Jewish problem. "...Nathan, I want to live in Christendom and become an aristocrat...wash away the Jewish stain" (170). Zuckerman the writer is a prophet of assimilation. He has (at least one) follower, who takes his fiction literally. It corresponds to the idea of American Jewish fiction as religious holy writing: people follow it. When Jimmy starts to take out the gun he is knocked out by Israeli security agents, both he and Zuckerman are handcuffed. He lies that Zuckerman is his father. One of the agents shows Zuckerman a knife used for circumcision in the old Galicia: "Our best *mohels* today are trained killers"(176).

In the new Israel the antiterrorist agent is given a knife, which used to serve in a religious ritual, and in a way their activity is the continuation of that ritual. Circumcision provides the spiritual survival connecting the Jews to the covenant and the agents provide for the safety. The agent who calls himself "a simple guy" has made aliya from Cleveland. He continues the previous discussion and has the ultimate answer to Jimmy's idea of Holocaust being the source of Antisemitism. He thinks that the most Gentiles

> ...confronted with the Holocaust, don't really give a shit. We don't have to shut down Yad Vashem to help them forget – they forgot...What is it they want to know...how long are these Jews going to go wailing on about their little Holocaust?...This didn't happen to one poor little saint

two thousand years ago – *this happened to six million living people only the other day!...* Everybody thought they were poor helpless shnooks...But suddenly, these duplicitous Jews...defeat their three worst enemies, wallop the shit out of them in six fucking days, take over the entire this and the whole of that, and what a shock!" (Roth, 178-180)

As the plane returns to Israel instead of continuing to London because of the accident, Zuckermann finds himself "shackled to God's bird, the El Al plane...being lectured on... the goy's half-hidden, justifiable fear of wild, belated Jewish justice"(181). A plane which flies an Israeli company and has a Star of David on its wings, belongs to God's aviation by definition. A plane represents shifting of identity, it literally crosses borders, countries, cultures and even languages, but an El Al plane is different. Zuckerman cannot escape because he is literally shackled to the Jewish plane. It seems Israel does not let go easily even of a Jew who moves to England and marries an aristocrat.

For many Jews of the younger generation, Germany is connected to feelings of guilt, like in Jenna Kalinsky's essay in The Modern Jewish Girl's Guide to Guilt, titled "Great, my Daughter is Marrying a Nazi." It describes the guilt feelings of a Jewish girl who married a German and went with him to live in Germany. Her family was not very observant, they had Hebrew school and bat mizvahs, and as a matter of practicality, Hannukklaus came "as a one-shot deal" on December twenty-fifth. But there were two issues from which there was no deviation, they had a weight of commandments: "First: never have anything to do with Germany, its people, culture or commerce. Second: marry the one you love – as long as he is Jewish" (Kalinsky, 231). When she comes to Germany she is confronted with the war photos of Jewish roundups which hang on the slats of a simulated cattle car in the public square. In America she was a person whose identity consisted of many things: being a woman, American, Jewish, but here only one part of her identity stands out. She feels she is

suddenly loved too much, like a bear squeezed until the stuffing leaks out. Once it was in the open, typical Germans my age flushed through a rainbow of contorted facial expressions and stammerings to express their contrition, to connect. In the end it was always: Oh, I know someone who works at the Jewish Museum in Frankfurt...A woman in my mother's book club knows someone who is Jewish! (238)

For Kalinsky, Germany is marked by its history. In her personal history she struggles with the past in her present. She writes that she taught English at the former Zyclon B industrial plant, to think of which which makes her uncomfortable. She feels "utterly other" and in the end even moving to Canada does not help to keep her family together.

Tova Reich makes a macabre connection between Germany and death in the Jewish War. The main protagonists Hoshea and Yehudi are flying to Israel hidden in coffins during the Six Day War because there is no regular air traffic to Israel except for burials. They are witnessing how a coffin of the Holocaust survivor who wanted to be buried in the Holy land, falls out of the plane in a turbulence. Yehudi decides they must be over the German territory.

> When these two dead Jews, may they rest in peace, hit that polluted ground, with their blue numbers tattooed on their forearms, those Nazis will know that we haven't finished with them yet. It will be for them a sign from above that they'd better watch their heads. Dead Jews will come pouring down upon them form the sky, and, like the evildoers of the generation of Noah, they will perish in the deluge! (Jewish War, 54)

As they peer out of the door which swung open they see the ground down below. Hoshea is suddenly overwhelmed by the shocking realization: "It could have been one of us!" (54). His friend Yehudi answers: "that's exactly the point. Then and now, it could have been one of us. And we must never forget it!" (55). By "then" he means during the Nazi time, although they had not been born then. According to the Jewish tradition, every Jew is obligated to feel as if he or she went out of Egypt, Exodus being the formative event in the history of Jewish people. Here the formative event is the Holocaust. And indeed they had been over Germany when the coffin fell out.

> Hoshea read an item in an old newspaper some weeks later about a coffin that had hurtled down from an overflying plane and struck the thatched roof of a gingerbread cottage with potted geraniums in window boxes in the Black Forest, and had landed at the feet of a blond woman in a dirndl skirt and a blond man in lederhosen, miraculously killing only a dog named Putzi. (55)

Of course, this is a parody on a stereotype of Germany, almost from a Grimm brothers' fairy tale. The romanticized German blond family is wearing national costumes and lives in a gingerbread cottage in Black Forest. The dog, in this case a harmless victim, evokes associations with the German shepherd dogs who accompanied the Nazi criminals when they were murdering their victims. When it was revealed that it was indeed over Germany that the coffin dropped,

"...Hoshea thought that his friend was seeking to attribute a higher purpose and design, some sort of message-bearing mission, to so seemingly brutal and grotesque a fate for two old Jews who had suffered more than their share in their lifetimes and who, in all justice, should have been laid to rest gently instead of hurtled from the sky" (55).

When seeking for a higher purpose of the Holocaust, many Orthodox religious leaders attribute it to the sins the Jews committed against God, like assimilation and turning back from the tradition. They claim that the Nazis were the instrument of God's wrath against His people. The parallel Reich uses shows how futile is the attempt to try to find a reason for events which cannot be explained by reason or logic.

Here the connection between the Holocaust, America and Israel is especially underscored, when the characters fly in coffins from America over Germany to Israel. All these locations are interconnected through the Jewish history and religion. God promised the return of the exiled and the coming of the Messiah – and Yehudi is a messianic figure in the novel, connected to Hebron where the Patriarchs of the Jewish people are buried. His name "Ha Goel" means saviour in Hebrew (but is not translated in the novel).

4. Language

Language is connected to both religious and ethnic dimensions of Jewish identity. For many centuries, Jews have been living in a multilingual situation. They could speak several languages: the liturgical Hebrew, the spoken Jewish language and the language of the non-Jewish environment. The Hebrew alphabet is a significant component of Jewish linguistic identity. It is used for several Jewish languages besides Hebrew, like Yiddish, Judeo-Arabic and Ladino.

In America, Yiddish, "the mother tongue" or *mameloshn,* is associated with ancestry, and Hebrew, the holy tongue, is associated with religion.

Hana Wirth-Nesher points out, that multilingualism has always characterized Jewish civilization. She quotes Baal-Makhshoves, who observed as early as 1918, that the mark of Jewish literature had always been its bilingualism, tracing the bilingual status back to the Bible (Call it English, 6). Although the native language in which modern Jewish American writers write is English, Jewish languages are used in many works of contemporary literature, connecting the characters to their heritage and their religious or ethnic identity.

4.1 Hebrew

Hebrew is the language of religious practice. A Jewish believer needs to learn it in order to be able to pray and recite the Torah. Hebrew is an official language of the State of Israel. The establishment of the State of Israel made Hebrew the national language, and interest in studying it rose among many American Jews. It also serves as a lingua franca between the Jews from different communities.

According to Hana Wirth-Nesher, in the context of religious practice, the only language that has been a continuous integral feature of Jewish life no matter what the country of origin for Jews has been Hebrew. At rites of passage in the life of an individual Jew and at communal observance of rituals, Hebrew prayers are recited and heard ("Traces," 119-120). Just as Israel is an important part of Jewish identity, Hebrew plays a central role as well.

Anne Roiphe thinks that after prayer and remembering, the third component of the Jewish experience is language. "The Hebrew sounds and the Hebrew rhythmic pattern seem special, mysterious and of a great and ancient beauty." (195) There is a difference, though, between the status and attitude toward the Hebrew language in America and in Israel.

In Israel, Hebrew is as plain as any other language, but in America, "...Hebrew sounds profound, sad, magical...Hebrew, like Latin, seems to be truer, purer, because it began closer to the beginning of things" (195).

Interesting to note that Latin, which is connected to Roman Catholic tradition has "holy" connotations for Roiphe, when it is in fact, the language of the conquerors of Jerusalem, who were the reason Jews had been exiled.

According to Hana Wirth-Nesher, Hebrew is a sign of an even older identity than Yiddish of one's grandfathers, a sign "not of family history but of ancient history, not of relatives but of ancestors" (Call it English, 1).

She points out that the linguistic story of Jewish American writing has been in large part, "a passage out of Yiddish, the language of immigrants, and a passage into Hebrew, the language of religious rites..." (3).

Hebrew usually appears in works of American Jewish literature in the form of scripture, liturgy and hermeneutic texts.

Hebrew is more than just a language. The Scripture was written in Hebrew, it is the language of creation of the universe, according to Jewish religious belief.

It reminds of the past and unites the Jewish history with the messianic future in the Land of Israel, where it is spoken again.

Ellen Uffen notes that in Ozick's Puttermesser Papers, Puttermesser invents her past in the form of Uncle Zindel, who teaches her Hebrew. "Puttermesser understands the ancient language as much more than a simple tie to the Jewish past from her place in history. She is in love with the gorgeous permutations of Hebrew grammar." She believes that knowledge of Hebrew will allow her to understand the workings of the universe (125). In "Puttermesser: Her Work History" Puttermesser studies Hebrew because she is sure it is a code for the world's design. According to Susanne Klingenstein, Ozick thinks of Hebrew "not only as the vessel and vehicle of Israeli culture but also of Jewish moral ideas and principles of civilization." Because ancient and modern Hebrew are recognizably continuous, Hebrew is assigned the function of a "unifying substratum," linking widely dispersed Jewish cultures temporally and spatially in one Jewish people. The language of the Diaspora Ozick considers "perishable" tongues, whereas Hebrew was the "language of perpetuation" ("In Life I am not Free," 57). Hebrew serves as a bond that ties the past and future together and the place too (Israel).

The sound of Hebrew can make a person return to religion. In Roth's Counterlife, Zuckerman's brother has a life-changing experience when he hears children in ultra Orthodox neighborhood of Mea Shearim chanting in Hebrew, a language he is unable to understand or read. "Children chanting away in Hebrew, I couldn't understand a word of it, couldn't recognize a single sound, and yet I was listening as though something I didn't even know I'd been searching for was suddenly reaching out for me" (Roth, Counterlife, 60).

The sound of Hebrew makes him realize, "I am not just a Jew, I'm not also a Jew -- I am a Jew as deep as those Jews. Everything else is nothing"(61).

His genetic memory of Hebrew makes him return home, to the land of the forefathers of the Jewish people, abandoning his life of complacency and materialism in the New Jersey haven. He finds a sense of purpose by settling in the Jewish State. His encounter with his brother who wants to bring him to his sense, takes place in Hebrew *ulpan*, a language class, where new immigrants learn to speak, read and write the language. Most of them are from America, and Hebrew is their first step of return to their historical homeland.

Hebrew serves as a vital connection to the written tradition and the universal Jewish identity, uniting different groups of Jews who speak different languages but use Hebrew in liturgy.

In the Ashkenazic Jewish tradition, Hebrew is the language associated with the male world of religious learning. According to Naomi Seidman, the traditional community in Eastern Europe was multilingual and used two Jewish languages: Hebrew and Yiddish. The sphere of use for each of them was specific – Hebrew was the language of study and liturgy, whereas Yiddish was a spoken language of everyday life. Since studying religious texts was reserved for males, women as a rule did not know Hebrew. As Benjamin Harshav points out:

> Religious education and scholarship were predominantly for men, schools and study-houses were exclusively for men; teachers and preachers were male; boys accompanied their fathers to synagogue and absorbed expressions in Hebrew and Aramaic. The Holy Tongue became associated with the male world... Yiddish was the language of home, family events and intimacy. (23)

Hebrew as the language of prayer and learning was traditionally the realm of male scholars, whereas women's domestic world was traditionally defined by Yiddish.

4.2 Yiddish

Yiddish is the language that European (Ashkenazic) Jews used for everyday communication, for some prayers and for secular literature.

Since most of the American Jews today are of Eastern European origin, Yiddish plays an important role in their writing.

Because of the great size of immigration from Eastern Europe in the beginning of the twentieth century, Yiddish became the main language of American Jewry. The preceding waves of Jewish immigration by Sephardim in 17th and 18th centuries and the German Jews in the 19th century were considerably smaller. The Jewish American literature in its present form is mostly shaped by the group of immigrants using Yiddish. In late nineteenth-century Europe and in America, Yiddish was more than a means of communication, it clearly marked the ethnic identity of its speakers (Fischer, 212-213).

Compared to high prestige of English, Yiddish had had a low status, considered by many "a jargon," or a mongrel language consisting of Hebrew, German and Slavic components.

> The accusation that Yiddish was an inferior dialect was not only levelled against it from outside the Jewish community but also from inside. In eastern Europe it was particularly the Jewish enlightenment, the *Haskalah*, that looked on the language with disdain... The Yiddish tradition was an oral one and the use of Yiddish as a literary language still relatively new. (Fischer, 215)

According to Jeffrey Shandler, many American Jews in the postwar years were embarrassed by Yiddish and saw it as a vestige of immigrant difference. The topic of the neglect of Yiddish appeared in American Jewish literature after the Holocaust and as it was becoming a lost language, at the same time it was gaining a new value as a signifier of loss of it speakers in the Holocaust. Shandler points out that the sudden absence of Yiddish speech became "a compelling metonym for the tragic loss of its speakers." "Devotion to Yiddish as an act of remembrance and of defiant Jewish persistence in the face of genocide" makes its role significant and does not let it disappear (Shandler, 18-19).

In Dara Horn's novel The World to come, a character who speaks Yiddish leads an inner dialog with another non-Yiddish speaking character who claims: "What's really interesting about Yiddish...is how much humor there is in it" (13). Yiddish was associated with popular culture and its cultural significance has been reduced to comedy and humor.

> ...what it really does have...what you don't know it has, because it isn't in any Woody Allen movies -- is a world of the dead built into it, a true fear of heaven, an automatic need to invoke the presence of God whenever saying anything good or bad about anyone or anything, an absolute trust

in the other world, if one could call it that, is not separate from this one,
that eternity is always breathing over your shoulder... (13)

According to H. Wirth-Nesher, the Holocaust is still considered the turning
point for the representation of Yiddish in Jewish American literature
("Accented Imagination," 291). After the Holocaust, when most speakers of
Yiddish were eliminated, it started taking on the traits of Hebrew in its role as
a sanctified language of dead martyrs. Therefore, it functions as a language of
a culture that does not exist anymore; there is something nostalgic in writing
about it.

Yiddish becomes holy because it reminds of the lost Jewish culture,
perished to religious and ethnic persecution. It is connected to history, to the past,
thus, in a sense taking the function of Hebrew as the holy language. In Horn's
passage, it invokes the idea of God's presence in the world by creating a
connection to eternity. Pascal Fischer claims that after the Holocaust and the
founding of the Jewish State, the functions of Hebrew and Yiddish have changed
considerably. "Yiddish was increasingly associated with the victims of the
Holocaust while Hebrew – apart from retaining its religious meaning – became
linked with the image of the self-assured Israeli" (220).

After its rebirth in Israel, Hebrew became the every-day language of
communication, and Yiddish, the traditional vernacular became sanctified
through the martyrdom of the six million speakers who are forever muted and
whose culture is lost for the world. Fischer quotes Cynthia Ozick's letter, where
she observes that "murdered Yiddish begins to take on some of the holiness of
liturgy and hallowed Hebrew becomes workaday mamaloshen" (222).

Sometimes the knowledge of Yiddish is reduced to a few words, it is the
last vestige of Jewishness, a connection to the Eastern European immigrant
world.

J. Foer's American protagonist is teaching his new Ukrainian friend Yiddish in
a funny dialog:

> Shtetls. A shtetl is like a village...It's a Jewish word...Yiddish. Like
> schmuck. "What does it mean schmuck?" "Someone who does
> something that you don't agree with is a schmuck." "Teach me another."
> "Putz." "What does it mean?" "It's like schmuck." "Teach me another."
> "Schmendrik." "What does it mean?" "It's also like schmuck." "Do you
> know any words that are not like schmuck? " He pondered for a
> moment. "Shalom"..."which is actually three words, but that's Hebrew,

not Yiddish. Everything I can think of is basically schmuck.
(Illuminated, 60)

Sadly, the modern American Jewish protagonist has an extremely limited
Yiddish vocabulary, it is limited to a few obscene and funny words, many of
which entered the mainstream American English. The shtetl, which does not
exist anymore, is one word connecting Jonathan to his Eastern European Jewish
past.

Many writers who wrote about immigrant experience have tried to represent
Yiddish speech in English text. Fischer gives an example of Sidney Nyburg, who
uses indirect speech in order to represent Yiddish conversation and tells the
readers that the original language was Yiddish. Nyburg was a German Jew, not
too familiar with the language of the eastern European Jews, who adopted a role
of cultural and linguistic interpreter for implied German-Jewish readers. Another
case of Yiddish speech in translated form is The Rise of David Levinsky, where
Abraham Cahan renders Yiddish as Standard English direct speech.

Most of the writers translate into a kind of English, which reminds
readers of the source language. Direct speech passages are interspersed with a
few Yiddish words, interjections like *nu, ach, Oi wei* or lexical words
expressing concepts which come form the Jewish culture like *shadkhan* (a
marriage broker), *cheder* (Hebrew primary school). Sometimes transliterated
lines of Yiddish are inserted (Fischer, 216-17).

Michael Chabon creates a utopic Yiddishland in The Yiddish Policemen's
Union. Similar to the early immigrant novels, the Yiddish speech in this book is
reproduced in standard English. English speech is marked and called "speaking
in American." The American Jews are called "Mexicans" and the Sitka Jews
"The frozen chosen." In the novel's content the State of Israel had been
destroyed the moment it appeared. In this fictional world, Yiddish is the winner
in the language competition with its rival Hebrew.

In fact, Hebrew has different pronunciations of the same spelling.
Ashkenazi Hebrew pronunciation was formed in Central and Eastern Europe and
survived in Orthodox communities until the present. (Harshav, Language, 153)
The modern Hebrew, spoken in Israel, has the traditional Sephardic
pronunciation. One of the reasons to have chosen it was that the reviver of
Hebrew Eliezer Ben Yehuda and the Hebrew Language Counsil associated the

Ashkenazic accent with ghetto, exile and Yiddish, the despised language of the Exile (Fellman 84, Seidman 113). The stereotype of Yiddish being a perverted language, reflecting the perversion of the soul of the Diaspora Jew, first formulated most harshly by Moses Mendelssohn, was as relevant for Ashkenazi Hebrew. It was also used for Rabbinic and Hasidic writings in which the Hebrew spelling was influenced by semi-spoken language and often disregarded Hebrew grammar. The Zionist government inherited the revulsion toward Rabbinic and Hasidic Hebrew, "especially in its wish to skip two thousand years of history and return to the wholesome Bible" (Harshav, Language, 157).

But in Chabon's novel the situation is reversed. In the war between the languages, Yiddish is the winner and Hebrew is associated with failure – the destruction of the Israeli State in 1948 in the novel's content. The suspects who plot blowing up the Dome of the Rock in order to hasten the coming of Messiah, speak Israeli Hebrew.

> Landsman knows Hebrew when he hears it. But the Hebrew he knows is the traditional brand, the one his ancestors carried with them through the millenia of their European exile, oily and salty as a piece of fish smoked to preserve it, flesh flavoured strongly by Yiddish. That kind of Hebrew is never employed for human conversation. It's only for talking to God....it was not the old slat-herring toungue, but some spiky dialect, a language of alcali and rocks. It sounded to him like the Hebrew brought over by the Zionists after 1948. Those hard desert Jews tried fiercely to hold on to it in their exile but, as with the German Jews before them, got overwhelmed by the teeming tumult of Yiddish, and by the painful association of their language with recent failure and disaster...that kind of Hebrew is extinct except among a few last holdouts meeting annually in lonely halls. (Chabon, 286)

This reversal of linguistic reality makes the initiated reader imagine what could have happened if history had taken a different turn. In Chabon's novel, the kind of Hebrew Israelis speak did not survive the exile. The "real-world" language situation of Yiddish: annual meetings in "lonely halls" (which is not exactly true anymore because of revived interest to Yiddish culture) is projected onto Hebrew. In reality Yiddish was abandoned in Israel for the sake of Hebrew.

An effort to restore the neglected and forgotten Yiddish, to make it alive again can become comic. For Tova Reich Yiddish is "a language of atonement" for the sins of anti-Semitism. One character in Mara is a Ukrainian named Bogdan Chmielnicki,"... who wrote poems in Yiddish, a language he had taught himself with much difficulty in atonement for an ancestor's sin" (135). The name of Chmielnicki, who murdered a third of the Jewish population of Poland and Ukraine evokes associations with rabid hatred of Jews. It is not clear whether his namesake's learning Yiddish can atone for anything, but the character is trying – it is hardly possible to write poems in a language of hatred.

4.3 English

According to Hana Wirth-Nesher, Yiddish is the signifier of the Old World culture, Hebrew is connected with ancient identity, ancestral history and deeper roots, but the language that American Jews speak is English.

"Nowadays, the primary language of American Jewry is neither Yiddish nor Hebrew. Despite impressive bodies of literature in both of these languages produced in the United States, the language of American Jewry has become English, so much so that Cynthia Ozick has at one time suggested that English be referred to as New Yiddish..."(Call it English, 3).

For immigrants English was the "infallible sign of Americanization" (Fischer, 217). The process of learning English is a crucial step to become a full-fledged American, as shown in many works of immigrant literature.

Mary Antin declares her love for the English language. She describes how she learned English words in a poetic way, comparing words to blossoms: "Getting a language in this way, word by word, has a charm that may be set against the disadvantages. It is like gathering a posy blossom by blossom"(166).

She describes her problems with pronunciation and accent, which distinguish her from "native" Americans. "I remember to this day what a struggle we had over the word "water". Miss Dillingham and I. It seemed as if I could not give the sound of *w;* I said "vater" every time (165).

The "w" and "th" sounds were the "giveaways," and also appear in David Levinsky's story. In Abraham Cahan's novel, David Levinsky also describes the difficult process of language acquisition. "Some English words inspired me with hatred, as though they were obnoxious living things ...English impressed me as the language of a people afflicted with defective organs of speech. Or else it would seem to me that the Americans had normal organs of speech, but that they made special efforts to distort the "t" into a "th" and the "v" into a "w" (130, 133). Learning English has become an obsession in immigrant novels. Immigrants fervently believed that English was the ticket to successful Americanization and becoming an American meant a linguistic transformation (Wirth-Nesher, Call it English, 7).

Just a few decades ago the issue of correct English pronunciation was a source of mortification to the immigrants from Eastern Europe. Their body was indelibly branded with an accent, which they wanted to get rid of along with the languages and culture their accent represented. As Hana Wirth-Nesher remarks:

> ... Mary Antin could write, think, and dream in English, but when she spoke, she did so with an accent. Her body, the physical continuity that she asserted was no disadvantage in her conversion story, nevertheless constituted the obstacle to her complete transformation. For accent is the body remembering. The language into which she was born would inevitably leave its imprint...Detectable physical difference, evident in Antin's speech, is what she feared could prevent her from passing in society...Like the Ephraimites in the Book of Judges who knew the password that could save them, but were prevented from passing over the river into safety because they could not pronounce the first consonant of *shibboleth, s*o the immigrant Mary Antin could not pass over in speech..." (Call it English, 56)

Antin and Cahan, whose native language was not English, chose to write in it partly to reach their Gentile audience and partly to prove to themselves that they mastered the new language. Rose Cohen's less famous autobiography, which was first published in 1918 and reissued in 1995, was written in an English language class. It was a kind of exercise which helped her master the language.

In modern novels, the "backward assimilation" concerns accent and language as well. The characters want to return to their ancestral roots and they even want to un-Americanize their accents. In Tova Mirvis's Outside World, a newly orthodox character Shayna, who used to be Susan, wants to "pass" in her neighbourhood as a "native." She is eager to assimilate into her new environment in a sealed-off community. "Shayna hoped to seal herself off from her past, so that no one would know... She had acquired a slight Brooklyn accent, and she sprinkled her sentences with bits of Hebrew and Yiddish...The bookshelves were lined with Hebrew books" (Mirvis, 15).

In Tova Reich's Jewish War Emunah, formerly Faith, an American who came to Israel to fulfill the commandment to settle the Land of Israel, speaks English at an Arab market with a young Arab, who "refused to understand the tongue of the occupier." (Reich, 7) Though Emunah is an American girl from Flatbush,

> her English was now dented and stamped with a variety of accent and syntax that could only be placed elsewhere, somewhere aromatically foreign, but nowhere on a physical map that you could put your finger on...It rendered her exotic, no longer just another predictable girl from Brooklyn, and placed her in a community of romantic exiles,...people with a story. (7)

She is no longer a "normal" American, she shows her "foreignness" to American materialistic values by means of her exotic accent. But in Hebrew, she has a "bland American accent" too, "so it was as if Emunah HaLevi possessed only accents and no native language at all" (Reich, 8). As hard as she tries, her accent marks her as an outsider and there is no place she is home at -- not in America, and not in Israel either. She tries to establish a connection with her roots by living in Israel, but she can never really be at home there, since she is an American, even though she left America behind. She has no home, her accent forever marking her as an outsider.

In <u>Master of the Return</u>, Bruria Lurie also cannot get rid of her Americanness: "Poor Bruria...she could never completely shake off the bland shadow of the American girl she had been, which lingered in her voice and her gestures, trivializing the personage she had become, rendering her slightly synthetic" (Reich, 53).

Now the situation of immigrants to America is reversed, and it is the American accent and body language which is a source of mortification for the newly religious characters, who cannot get rid of it.

4.4 Name and Identity

The contemporary writers' choice of name or language preference of their characters is not accidental. Names have served as an important identity marker throughout the Jewish history. When early immigrants came to the United States, they often had their names changed, mainly for the sake of convenience, in order to become Americanized. For example, Mary Antin describes how the family chose their new American names, getting rid of the old ones together with the old clothing.

> With our despised immigrant clothing we shed also our impossible Hebrew names. A committee of our friends, several years ahead of us in American experience, put their heads together and concocted American names for us all...My mother, possessing a name that was not easily translatable, was punished with the undignified nickname of Annie. Fetchke, Joseph and Deborah issued as Frieda, Joseph, and Dora, respectively. (149)

Rose Cohen has her name changed from Rachel to Ruth, which is a biblical name also, but is familiar to protestant Gentiles. Her aunt Masha becomes Jenny. Since Rose is more Americanized than her father and "under pressure" can "converse" in English, it is her task to translate her siblings' names. The name Ezekiel she changes into Morgan simply because she likes to have an uncommon name for her brother (Cohen, 182).

Anne Roiphe tells in her autobiography how her mother told her the story of the family name secret. The mother was forbidden to pronounce the name they had in Europe, which she accidentally overheard from her aunts when she was a small child. After coming to America, it had been changed to Phillips and her aunts admonish her: "If you ever tell anyone the name... your children and your children's children will be cursed with disease and pain, misfortune and early death. If you tell this secret to any of your older sisters or brothers, their children too will die in agony. Not a soul must know the name of our family before we came to America" (15). When her mother was dying, Roiphe was imploring her to reveal the secret: "If you don't tell me perhaps no one will ever know" (16). But her mother refuses, fearing that she might bring the curse on her daughter's family. The past had been cut off so completely that it was strictly forbidden even to mention the old name under a threat of a biblical curse. The name disappears because no one knows and remembers it, obliterating a family history.

Eva Hoffman writes her autobiography in the 1960's, when her family flees anti-Semitic Poland. But still the name change is a necessary measure. It is done quickly and easily.

> Mine -- Ewa"-- is easy to change into its near equivalent in English, "Eva." My sister's name -- "Alina"-- poses more of a problem, but after a

moment's thought, Mr. Rosenberg and the teacher decide that "Elaine" is close enough. My sister and I hang our heads wordlessly under this careless baptism...

Our Polish names didn't refer to us; they were as surely us as our eyes or hands. These new appellations, which we ourselves can't yet pronounce, are not us. (105)

Ewa's sister Alina is named after their mother's sister, who perished in the Holocaust. Together with her name, the memory of her aunt is lost, too. Eva calls this procedure "a baptism," which calls to mind the forced conversions in the Middle Ages, when the choice was either a new religion and identity or death.

When immigrants come to Israel, they undergo a name change too. Their American Jewish names are Hebraized. The change from Yiddish to Hebrew names had a long tradition, it was a "normal" practice for early Zionists, entailing a fundamental self-transformation from Diaspora Jews to Israelis. The names of central Biblical figures, popular in Yiddish, seemed too Jewish and were exchanged for names from nature, "meaningful" names like "Light", "Joy", or names of unfavourable Biblical characters that were not widespread in European Jewry. Hebrew words identified with Yiddish words were also rejected (Harshav, Language, 167). "The Hebraizing of diaspora names can be traced to the old Jewish custom of changing the name of a very sick man in the hope of cheating the angel of death...Jewish refugees... have shown a proclivity to redefine themselves with names that denote firmness, strength, courage, and vigour:...Oz ("strength"); ... Lahat ("blaze")...Barak ("lightning")" (Elon, The Israelis qtd in Seidman, 117).

Hebrew names symbolize liberty, freedom from the ghetto and independent statehood. In Marge Piercy's He She and It, the Jewish characters have Hebrew names, which are not translated for a non-Hebrew speaking reader. Shira, Malka, Gadi are Israeli names, but the novel's setting is not Israel, it is a free town of Tikva, which is situated on the former East Coast of the United States. Tikva is a full and active democracy. "...the foundation of Tikva was libertarian socialism with a strong admixture of anarcho-feminism, reconstructionist Judaism (although there were six temples, each representing a different Jewishness) and greeners" (Piercy, 404). Hebrew names give Tikva residents their Jewish identity, and the name of the town means hope in Hebrew, hope for the future and for continuity. Israeli names are associated with the notion of Israeli Jew, who is free, has no fear of pogroms and is capable of defending himself.

In Tova Reich's Jewish War, Yehudi Ha Goel had been Jerry Goldberg in the United States. Emunah, the wife of Yehudi's closest friend and right hand had been Faith, Herbie becomes Hoshea. The changing of names is connected to the idea of rebirth in the new homeland. Other newly orthodox characters also have their names Hebraized. Like Mary Antin and early immigrants who Americanized their names, here in the process of rebirth, the characters shed their Yiddish Diaspora Jewish names and take the "proud" Hebrew ones.

In Tova Mirvis' The Outside World the main character's mother, Shayna Goldman, used to be Susan Cantor. Susan took a Yiddish name, which reconnects her to the Eastern European Orthodox shtetl past.

Her future son in law, Bryan, is becoming more and more religiously observant. He comes from a religious orthodox family, but after having spent two years in Israel in a yeshiva his family's modern Orthodoxy is not religious enough for him.

> ...he came home and informed them that he no longer wanted to be called Bryan. He wanted to use his Hebrew name, Baruch, which they had given him in memory of Joel's grandfather. But they had never intended it for the outside world. Because Baruch carried with it the dreaded *ch* , the modern-day shibboleth...Not a Ch as in Charlie, not a Sh as in Shirley, but a guttural sound that came from the back of those throats that had been trained to utter it from birth. (Mirvis, 28)

Yiddish sound becomes the sound of "passing" into the old culture, the culture which Bryan-Baruch is desperately trying to return to. Mirvis uses the word "shibboleth" which Hana Wirth-Nesher uses to describe the impossibility of Mary Antin's linguistic passing into America (Call it English, 56). Now it is used for "passing out" of America. "...Bryan had taken this far too seriously and searched for roots that went deeper than Laurelwood, New Jersey, where they lived. Their son wanted to pass through Ellis Island in reverse, to find a Poland, a Lithuania, a Galicia, he was sure still existed somewhere" (Mirvis, 29).

When Brian's father Joel looks at the family pictures of his Lithuanian grandparents, he realizes that he doesn't know anymore if he sees the past or the future.

All he knew was that they were the last European generation in his family...In just a few generations, his family had become American. Joel had once thought of these photographed ancestors as the last of their kind, a remnant of a world that once existed. Now he wondered who would outlast whom. His family had come forward and now they were boomeranging backward. (Mirvis, 95)

Hebrew names mean loyalty to religious and cultural heritage, they are signs of refusal to assimilate. In Marge Piercy's novel, in the corporate culture of Y-S where they live, the main character Shira and her Israeli-born husband Josh are called *marranos*. It is a Spanish term meaning "pig," which had denoted Spanish Jews, who were made to become Christians in times of the inquisition. Using allusion to a real historical fact creates an impression of continuity of Jewish history.

Being a mother is a very important part of Shira's life and also an important part of a Jewish tradition. She had her baby by natural birth, that is why she is considered "archaic" – corporate term used in personnel for people who were considered not quite civilized. In her personal file, she and her husband were labeled "culturally-retentive." "Shipman has difficulty assimilating beyond superficial level. Importance was attached to the name they had given their son. Hebrew name"(He, She and It, 280). Retaining a Hebrew name means attachment to their culture—it is a source of suspicion for the multi, which wants to control its workers completely. Stripping a person of a name means taking away his or her identity, their origin. A name can be a last string of attachment to the tradition of the fathers -- or, as in Shira's case, the tradition of the grandmothers.

The use of Jewish languages, names and Hebrew alphabet in works of American Jewish literature cannot be underestimated. Even the Hebrew letters have become "icons of Jewish religious and cultural tenacity" (Wirth-Nesher, "Accented Imagination," 295). The sound and the look of Hebrew or Yiddish, even if incomprehensible to both the character and the reader, marks the connection to Judaism in an English text.

5. Jewish tradition and feminism in women's writing

In traditional Judaism, the role of a woman has been limited to domestic sphere. Women are not allowed to study holy texts on equal terms with men. The role of a Jewish woman was that of a wife and a mother. The biggest reward was to have a husband and sons who are Torah scholars. This situation was not satisfying and many women decided they wanted a change because they felt they could not realize themselves as human beings inside the tradition. When in the second half of the twentieth century, the religious revival began, many women returned to Judaism in a new role as active members of the community, who made a difference in Jewish religious life. Since 1972 over a hundred female rabbis have been ordained in Reform and Reconstructionist movement of Judaism. The Conservative movement voted in 1983 to allow ordination of women. Many contemporary Jewish women have achieved a greater knowledge of the Hebrew language and Jewish texts, and have created new rituals, stories and blessings that connect their religious faith and spirituality to the realities of their everyday lives (Umansky, 281-85).

This tendency is reflected in Jewish American literature. Bible stories often portray women warriors and wise women who have names and their own voices. But later in history, the rabbinical culture became a purely male culture written by men for men. Rachel Biale quotes Talmud Berakhot 17 a, where women's role is discussed. "Women gain their merit by enabling and encouraging their husbands and sons to study the Torah" (39). A role model and an example of self-sacrifice is Rachel, the wife of the famous scholar Rabbi Akiva, who spent twenty-four years waiting for her husband who had gone to study. The tragic story of Bruria, the only Talmud scholar in the Talmud is an example of attitude to women's intellectual endeavours. Bruria is seen as a competitor and a threat to male authority. In Rashi's commentary, the end of the story is tragic. In order to prove that the dictum that women are tempting is right, Bruria's husband Meir commands one of his students to seduce her. Eventually, she commits suicide. There is a direct connection between learning and frivolity.

Rachel Adler states that women have the same legal status as children and slaves, being unable to bear witness in a Jewish court. "Teaching, the fundamental method of the Jewish people for transmitting religious insights, was closed to women...Woman's meager *mitzvoth* are...connected to some physical goal or object." The prayers for women were written in Yiddish because they were unable to understand Hebrew liturgy. The female mind was viewed as frivolous, all women as potential adulteresses. Adler calls Jewish women "a golem who did her master's will" (16-17). As one of Tova Reich's male characters puts it: "The role of a woman is to wail at funerals...not to blab" (Reich, Master, 80).

Anne Roiphe mentions a quote from the Jerusalem Talmud, tractate Sotah, chap. 3, sec. 4, where Rabbi Eliezer Hyrramus proclaims "Let the words of the Torah be burned rather than entrusted to women" (200). The prayer book has the blessing thanking God for "not having made me a woman" standing next to thanking "for not having made me a slave." It is not surprising then that contemporary Jewish women are resolved to change the situation. But is it possible to be a Jew and a feminist at the same time? And as a writer, how does one write within a heritage that traditionally disqualifies women as powerful beings?

For immigrant writers, the religious tradition has been associated with discrimination of women, it is seen as patriarchal and purely negative. The typical examples are Anzia Yezierska's Bread Givers or Mary Antin's Promised Land, where religious tradition is seen as the patriarchal vestige of the old world. The New World brings liberation of women from the patriarchal tradition, but at the same time from any kind of religious affiliation. Mary Antin describes America as the land, which gives women opportunities they could never dream of in the old world. In the old World section of her book, she describes how life was divided between Jews and Gentiles and also between boys and girls. When a boy started learning he became a hero of his family, he was "...praised, and blessed, and made much of. No wonder he said, in his morning prayer, " I thank Thee, Lord, for not having created me a female." It was not much to be a girl, you see. Girls could not be scholars and rabbonim." This was the way the Old world worked, where "a girl's real schoolroom was her mother's kitchen... of course, every girl hoped to be a wife. A girl was born for no other purpose" (Antin, 29). And yet, Antin felt she was a princess, "an heir to the centuries-old tradition, indestructible and proud...I heard the names of Rebecca, Rachel and Leah as early as the names of father, mother, and nurse" (35). The names of foremothers of the Jewish people: Rebecca, Rachel and Leah underscore her legacy as a woman in the Jewish tradition.

> I was taught to call myself a princess, in memory of my forefathers who had ruled a nation. Though I went in disguise of an outcast, I felt a halo resting on my brow.
> Sat upon by brutal enemies, unjustly hated, annihilated a hundred times, I yet arose and held my head high, sure that I should find my kingdom in the end... God needed me and I needed Him...according to an ancient covenant between Him and my forefathers. (Antin, 35)

She uses biblical language when telling of her origins: "Hayyim begat Joseph, and Joseph begat Pinchus, my father" (37). It is the language of the English Bible and also a male genealogy. As a woman and a Jew, she had been an outsider in Russia and remained an outsider in America, though in a different form.

In America, everything is different: "A long girlhood, a free choice in marriage, and a brimful womanhood are the precious rights of an American woman" (218). Of course, the fate of hundreds of immigrant girls who were working long hours under inhumane conditions of workshops has nothing to do with "American" way. Mary's sister Frieda did not gain much because she came too late and her father put her to work out of necessity. Antin blames it on the influence of the Old World traditions with charming naivety. "The greater the pity...there was no one to counsel him to give America more time with my sister...In books...she might have found a better answer to the riddle of a girl's life than a premature marriage" (218).

For Anzia Yezierska's character in Bread Givers, Sara, all that which has to do with religion is reserved for men. She is bitter that her father is unhappy he had no sons: "a boy could say prayers after his father's death – that kept the father's soul alive for ever. Always Father was throwing up to Mother that she had borne him no sons to ne an honour to his days and to say prayers for him when he died" (9). The prayers of his daughters didn't count because God didn't listen to women. Heaven and the next world were only meant for men. Women could get into heaven because they were wives and daughters of men. Women had no brains for the study of God's Torah, but they could be the servants of men who studied the Torah. Only if they cooked for the men, and washed for the men, and didn't "nag or curse the men out of their homes; only if they let the men study the Torah in peace, then, maybe they could push themselves into Heaven with the men, to wait on them there" (Yezierska, 9-10).

For both Mary Antin and A. Yezierska, religion and patriarchality belong to the long list of negative remainders of the Old World, where women had no access to formal education and no way to escape; the only path open to them – is to become wives and mothers, not having their own destiny to choose. America brings them, as both Jews and women, a chance to be able to choose their destiny, even if the price is that of giving up their identity.

Today, negative stereotypes of Jewish women have become widely accepted as a part of the popular culture. As Anna P. Bumble points out, one of them is the stereotype of a Jewish American princess, which had been developed first by Henry Wouk in Marjorie Morningstar and by Philip Roth in Good-bye, Columbus (26). According to David Biale, the roots of the negative images of American Jewish women, the stereotype known as "Jewish American Princess," are found in rabbinic homily. The Talmud rabbinical ethic condemns women as "prisoners of their own biology, incapable of willed sexual restraint..." There is no point of teaching them the law and since it is only men who can learn to control themselves, the texts are directed to male scholars (57).

Many scholars think that the disparaging perceptions of young Jewish women derive from identity problems of Jewish male authors. As Riv-Ellen Prell points out:"These stereotypical women represent the anxiety, anger and pain of Jewish men as they negotiate an American Jewish identity" (qtd in Bumble, 27). Jewish women are seen as "guardians of tradition" and the religious intolerance of the outside world is internalized and channeled to aggravation against women.

The fascination with the non-Jewish blond woman, which is a common theme in many works of Jewish American fiction written by male authors, is also a part of their "inferiority complex." One of possible reasons is that the Orthodox Jewish tradition is matrilineal. A male Jew is therefore under more pressure to find a Jewish partner if he wants to have Jewish offspring. This can be also a source of indignation and revolt against the bitchy, evil and materialistic Jewish woman. Bumble points out that the Jewish women were pictured in works by American-Jewish male authors both as repositories of

Jewishness and as obstacles of Jewish men's achievement of their goals. The men who suffered from anti-Semitic attitudes "tried to counterbalance their alien status by diverting public attention from themselves and channeling the negative perception of Jewishness onto Jewish women" (Bumble, 27).

In Letting Go, Philip Roth's protagonist who is intermarrying despite his family protest, has full understanding and support of his uncle: " I'm you. Jewish girls devour you. Haven't I seen my friends go under? The wives can't walk upstairs. They need maids. They need vacations - once in August, then in January all over again...One Friday you come in the door and they got the candles going, and then you're really home" (Roth, 81). This picture illustrates the stereotype of a spoiled Jewish woman, who needs maids and vacations and who at the same time keeps the Jewish tradition by lighting holiday candles.

Today, many women writers rethink and reclaim the Jewish tradition in their writing. Women writers often focus on "recovery" of Judaism, but not in its patriarchal form; they reclaim the Jewish tradition and their rights as Jews. They invent female characters who have acquired a voice. Marge Piercy invents Chava, the great Maharal's granddaughter, in the parallel story about the Golem of Prague in He, She and It. After the death of her husband, Chava returned to Prague to her grandfather's house in order to work as his secretary and also as a midwife. She rejects all marriage proposals because she prefers independent life and intellectual activity. Women like Chava had difficulty adjusting to the demands of the society they lived in. There was no place for them in the tradition of the fathers.

> She is the person she wants at the center of her life...She craves the clear bright working place of the intellect... Women...are the soldiers of the flesh...she declines to serve in that army of procreation and daily reclamation every woman is raised to join. No man seems to understand that in offering marriage, he is asking her to cut off her head. How could she bear and raise children, run a household and also engage in intellectual labour, scholarship, religious thought? (Piercy, 370)

Tova Reich deals with sexism and feminism in the settler community as representative of Orthodox Judaism. She attacks the silencing of women in religious community, where only men count and have the right to speak or carry out religious services. In Master of the Return, she criticizes with bitter irony the religious women's situation in Judaism:

No outsider can understand the absolute beauty of the Jewish woman's position. To the outsider, it looks like we're downtrodden and oppressed, like we're low, lower than low. We eat the leftovers. We are barred from the study halls. We're regarded as inferior and unclean. We're excused or simply forbidden from performing many of the rituals and *mitzvot,* from studying the more complicated and interesting texts...

Who dares...to deny the glory of the Jewish woman...she, the domestic beacon, the unmatched administrator, who bears and raises the children, who manages the household, who goes out and earns a living to provide for her husband and family while he sits all day in the *kollel* and learns Torah!...as her husband grows in wisdom and in holiness, she, too, is elevated and exalted. He endows her with sanctity. From him she receives her spirituality... (156)

Reich shows how women are treated in an Orthodox religious community, and how such treatment is justified from an "insider" point of view.

In Jewish War, there is an example of silencing women in the naming of a child, Golana. Her mother Shelly is separated from her husband in protest, because he had taken a second wife, Carmela. He arranged to be called to the Torah the next day after the birth during Sabbath prayers at the Cave of Machpela,

...where he chanted the blessing, and without any prior consultation with anyone...he named his daughter Golana...Such a thing was unheard of! Even in the Bible, the naming was usually reserved for the mother who had travailed and borne the child. Everyone agreed that this was traditionally the mother's prerogative...
Mother Eve, Mother Sarah, Mother Leah, Mother Rachel – all of these mothers fashioned names for the babies they had borne to commemorate the moment in their lives. This was in the Bible, Yehudi's main source, the book on which he based his entire mission, the book on the strength of which he justified all of his mad escapades and all of his wild claims. (Jewish War, 91)

Shelly is deprived even of having the right to name her daughter, she has no voice or opinion. Her husband manipulates the Bible when it is convenient and has no qualms about doing what he wants. The Bible justifies everything he does, just or unjust.

In Jewish War, the women characters take part in a study group discussion. The group is called "Bible as Therapy," discussing women in the Bible. The women are called in the tradition "daughters, sisters, wives, mothers of men, for so were these women defined" (Reich, 205). This is a sad comment, for women are defined through men, having no names of their own, they are deprived of personalities. Women can discuss the Bible between themselves but are not allowed to voice their opinion in public discussion on equal terms with men. By letting the readers "eavesdrop" on their conversation, Reich lets them draw their own conclusions. The discussion is opened by Malkie, Hoshea's third wife. Emunah is nursing her son, who doesn't let her speak.

> Just like a man... he wants you all to himself... men have to be in complete control. They never let a woman talk. Just take a look at the Bible...When a woman speaks...it's connected with some business involving men, or an abject petition... Eve has a conversation, and what's her reward? Expulsion form Eden, painful childbirths, eternal dependency on a man...Miriam speaks, and all she gets for her trouble is a case of leprosy. Women's speech is by definition gossip. And Esther... has to get all dolled up in her absolute best, makeup, perfume, the works, just to appear before the stupid King and speak a few words, and..., if he's not in the mood to listen, he can slice off her head. (Reich, 208)

Malkie voices her disillusionment and frustration with the male religious world, where men have complete control and women have no right to speak out. But the key question comes from Emunah, who asks: "Are you saying...that the Bible is sexist?" (209). Shelly has the answer: "Of course, the Bible is sexist. It's not even a question... But so what?... What do such modern concepts signify in relation to so cosmic an entity as the Torah?" (Reich, 210). But it is not only women that the Bible treats badly, she goes on to say. "Thousands are slaughtered in a single afternoon, or wiped out by a plague or pestilence or the wrath of God. Everyone's life, male or female, is like spilled water"(210).

It seems that Reich voices here her concerns about the morality of religion in general. Human beings are sacrificed for the sake of some abstract idea. It may be true or not true that women suffer more, but here in Hebron, men, women and children are like fowl of atonement, fighting for an idea, for a noble cause, and one individual life is like "spilled water." Yehudi's daughter Golana is killed during a demonstration, his other daughter disappears, but it doesn't matter to him, he is fighting for his ideals. In the end, he leads his community to a mass suicide, to die like heroes of Massada – hence the allusion to the "Jewish War" of Josephus Flavius in the name of the novel. The idea of self-sacrifice for the sake of ideology contradicts the American value system based on individual pursuit of happiness.

Another critic of religious Orthodox treatment of women is Rebecca Goldstein, whose fiction represents the current Jewish renewal. Her heroines are intellectual women,who strive for a balance between Western civilization and their Jewish heritage, seeking spirituality and self-fulfillment, struggling with their ethnic heritage and religious ambivalence (Anne P. Ronell, 152-53).

In Mazel, Goldstein depicts three generations of Jewish women. The grandmother Sasha is an actress who came to stardom in a Yiddish theatre in prewar Poland. The mother Chloe is a professor of classical languages. The granddaughter Phoebe is a professor of mathematics at Princeton, specializing in the geometry of soap bubbles. She is the one who chooses the traditional way of life, starts keeping kosher and gets married in an orthodox way. Here, it is the grandmother who is rebellious against the traditional way of life and who refuses to wear a skirt on Shabbat, thus offending her granddaughter's in-laws. Neither she nor Chloe can understand Phoebe's new involvement with traditional Judaism. "I can't understand you! You're an educated woman! A professor! Why would you want to start up all over again with those old ways?" (338). For older women, education is incompatible with religious beliefs. History of women in Judaism is jokingly presented through the mind of the rebellious grandmother Sasha in a parody on a Talmudic discussion:

> ...most of those ancient "do's and don't's" had been fashioned by men to keep things their way...one of the Talmudic sages confiding to another on a slow day in Babylonia. Just between you and me, my wife's cleanliness leaves a little something to be desired. Do you think we can write in a law about women having to bathe at least once a month? Done! Answers his friend...Don't let it go any further, but my wife keeps the house like a pigsty...Let's write in a law that every spring the women have to give the house such a cleaning that not a crumb of bread lurks in any corner...Listen, says a third, who's been eavesdropping on the conversation. If you're smart, then, before you do another thing, you'll make a law that the women can't make any laws. Can't even study the laws! Can't even read the language in which the laws are written! (Goldstein, 19)

Phoebe reminds Sasha of her dead sister, Fraydel, who had committed suicide back in the shtetl of her youth. With age Phoebe looks more and more like her. Only for Fraydel, there was no way to combine education and the traditional way of life. If her marriage did not work out, she would have stayed an outcast, an alien body in the community, where women had only one call -- being a mother and a wife. Phoebe brings up the subject of a Hebrew name which has to appear on her marriage contract. "I thought, since my name means "shining" in

Greek, that maybe I should use the Hebrew equivalent" (350). Sasha suddenly enters the conversation: "I want you to use the name "Fraydel" for your *ketuba*" (351).

The connection to the past is established through the granddaughter who fulfills the dreams of her dead great-aunt.

Sasha is reminded of her parents when the men sing a Hebrew song about the woman of valor, which is sung every Shabbat in every Jewish Orthodox home throughout the generations, "...the very song that Sasha's father, Nachum used to sing every Friday night to Leiba" (354). She is involuntarily connected to her European past, which she had struggled to cast away. The initiated reader knows that the traditional song is a poem with which King Solomon concludes the book of Proverbs (Proverbs 31). According to tradition, it is sung on the evening of Shabbat by men only and praises the woman of valor who works day and night in order for her husband to be able to study and grow in spirituality. Sasha does not join the dancing crowd, surveying what she calls the "reshtetilization of America" (354). She is trying to find irony in the situation but does not succeed. She is talking in her mind to her deceased husband: "Our daughter and granddaughter, both of them so educated, one a professor at Columbia, the other a professor at Princeton: where is their cynicism?" (356). But she finds none. Everyone is taking the dancing very seriously. The university educated granddaughter is rejecting her feminist upbringing for the sake of Orthodox family values. Jason and Phoebe prepared a booklet explaining the Orthodox wedding ceremony. Goldstein gives her readers a chance to get acquainted with the rituals by describing them in great detail, and at the same time keeps her distance by reminding the reader twice in one paragraph that she is quoting from the booklet.

> Phoebe circled round Jason seven times, a number, explained the pamphlet, that alludes to many things, including the number of times in the Torah where it is written "... and when a man takes a wife." Two blessings over wine were made, one praising God for creating the vine, the other praising Him for giving us the holiness of marriage... Jason placed the ring on Phoebe's finger, saying in Hebrew, "Behold you are consecrated to me with this ring in accordance with the laws of Moses and Israel."
> The ketuba was read aloud in Aramaic, and then seven "honored guests" (according to the pamphlet) were called up, one by one, each to recite one of the seven blessings. And the Jason stamped on the glass that

symbolizes the destruction of Jerusalem, always remembered in even the happiest of moments. (353)

Goldstein reminds the reader that the ancient texts are read in Hebrew and Aramaic so only few of the guests would have understood the proceedings without the help of the pamphlet. The book ends with a wedding scene, which symbolizes the chain of generations. "And Sasha and Chloe and Phoebe were all dancing together, their arms linked around one another's waists...as they swirled in the circles drawn within circles within circles. And so it goes on, it goes on" (356-7). The wedding is photographed by some Japanese tourists as a typical American wedding to show their friends in Japan. It shows how Jewish tradition became a part of American culture, representing America to a foreign eye.

It is presented, perhaps, as an ironic take on how America cannot be represented by a Jewish author by other tools than seeing everything through the lense of Jewishness. As a Jewish author, Goldstein is kind of trapped in the same loop as her female characters, who cannot let go of religious traditions.

It might be not a mere coincidence that both Tova Reich and Rebecca Goldstein come from Orthodox families and have received Jewish religious education. Tova Reich descended from a long line of rabbis, she is a daughter of a rabbi and a sister to three rabbis (Kirschenbaum, 73). Goldstein comes from a cantor's family. She describes her father, known as "the *Tzaddik* of White Plains" as a saintlike figure. She also had to fight hard for her intellectual freedom (Ronell, 154-56).

Both Reich and Goldstein know exactly what they rebel against.

6. Food and ritual

It is needless to say that food plays an important role in many cultures. It is a part of a person's personality, one of the first things a person remembers about his or her childhood. Therefore, it is not coincidental that a common saying claims: "you are what you eat."

Food is a very important part of the Jewish tradition too.

> Food for Jews meant more than calories for survival. It transcended pleasure. For poor and rich, regardless of place and time, food in the Judaic system stood squarely at the center of the sacred zone...Food embodied a palpable manifestation of Jewish conceptions of divine will. It functioned as a blueprint for human relations instituted by texts considered the word of God, and buttressed by law. The Judaic system assumed that food contained within it manifestations of holiness... (Diner, Hungering, 150-51)

Eating is connected to ritual, every holiday involves a preparation of specific food which has its symbolic meaning. When Jews celebrate Purim they eat "ears of Haman" to commemorate the victory over Haman, the evil persecutor of the Jewish people. On Chanukah, potato pancakes for example, are made with oil and eaten to commemorate the miracle of oil burning in the Temple for eight days instead of one. On Passover, every item on the plate has its special symbolic meaning commemorating the Egypt exodus.

Sydney Weinberg has stated that in the United States, the synagogue has ceased to have a central role in Jewish life, and the immigrant mothers' preservation of the Sabbath and festival rituals through the traditional dishes they prepared, fulfills a function of transmitting the Jewish heritage and sense of identity to their children. The memories of their mothers' cooking is the last Jewish vestige to be retained by the most assimilated persons. Food is also the easiest point of entry into a culture (qtd in Cooper, 201).

For Jews, the dietary laws of *kashrut* are a very important part of religious worship. Keeping kosher is a major identity marker. In literary works of Jewish writers, eating kosher signifies the embracing of religious identity, whereas eating forbidden food signifies the abandoning of the tradition – together with names, language and culture.

Hasja Diner emphasizes the link between food and memory, culture and religion, showing the importance of food rituals in Eastern European Jewish life, and in what ways coming to America had changed the food habits of immigrants. For Eastern European Jews, the world was divided between the acceptable and the unacceptable, and there was no questioning of the validity of the system.

> Eastern European Jews lived in a world where food was sacred for all...
> Good food, particularly at holy times, enhanced sanctity...
> Food also made Jews different from their non-Jewish neighbors. By the laws of *kashrut*, they could not mix meat and dairy and could only eat meat of certain animals slaughtered according to specific standards.
> Eastern European Jews lived in a world shaped by love of food...
> Each holiday called for its own special dishes. (Hungering for America, 147-148, 154-155)

When the Eastern European Jewish immigrants came to America in the beginning of the twentieth century, they faced new hardships: on the one hand, now most of them weren't on the brink of starvation, on the other hand, many of them had to give up much of the religious observance, for example, when they were living outside of big communities like New York. There was a dilemma between "staying true" to the religiously acceptable food and the opportunity to taste the new, "forbidden" food, which also had the allure of a "forbidden fruit." By means of food, an immigrant could either strengthen or loosen ties with the group he or she belonged to. The immigrants saw the regular meals on their table as America's gift, America meant freedom and food,, but there was a big temptation not to adhere to the religious laws concerning food (Diner, 178-80).

The laws of *kashrut* functioned in the past to keep the Jews separate and apart from the outside world. In Eastern Europe they lived separately from the Gentile world, the Gentile food was repulsive and unattractive to them. But America has been attractive as a culture and society, and its food lured the newcomers. The immigrants cherished American ideas about individual choice, personal preference and limitless opportunities. These ideas clashed with the many limitations of *kashrut* (Diner, Hungering, 224).

"*Kashrut* became one of the most divisive issues in the American Jewish world, turning Jews against each other, sundering families...While some immigrants emphatically rejected traditional food restrictions, adopting the anti-religious sentiment of left-wing politics, most Jews tried to live with the sacred system" (Diner, Hungering, 180-81).

At the beginning of twentieth century children of immigrants had to make difficult choices because schools were a place "...where food challenged integration" (184). Diner quotes Dan Oren's book Joining the Club: A History of Jews and Yale, which tells a story of Abraham Alderman. He immigrated with his parents in the early twentieth century and attended Yale University. Once he accepted a professor's invitation to dine at his house, he was afraid of what would happen if he refused pork or shellfish (184).

This story reminds of Mary Antin's recounting of a dinner at her teacher's home. She describes how invited to a dinner by her beloved English teacher, she faces a dilemma. She wants to behave properly, be like everybody else, equal among equals. She is served pork, which is strictly forbidden by the Jewish law.

> It was Miss Dillingham, she who helped me in so many ways, who unconsciously out me to an early test, the result of which gave me a shock that I did not get over for many a day. She invited me for tea one day, and I came in much trepidation. It was my first entrance into a genuine American household; my first meal at a Gentile – yes, a Christian – board. Would I know how to behave properly? I do know know whether I betrayed my anxiety... All went well, until a platter was passed with a kind of meat that was strange to me. Some mischievous instinct told me that it was ham – forbidden food; and I, the liberal, the free, was afraid to touch it!... And to think that so ridiculous a thing as a scrap of meat should be the symbol and test of things so august! (197)

Mary Antin decides to eat more than anybody else at the table as a way of defying religion for the sake of free thought. Her liberal view of the world leaves no place for some archaic laws, but her religious upbringing makes it very difficult for her to overcome instinctive disgust. David Levinsky also faces a big test by eating with Gentiles. As Hana Wirth-Nesher puts it:"His trial by fire will be the dinner table, where Gentile middle-class manners require soft tones and immobile limbs." It is tremendously important that he seeks out "... a culinary tutor so that he can read American menus" (Call it English, 11-12).

If early immigrants in the 19th century abandoned kosher food, the characters in contemporary novels often rebel in the opposite direction and start keeping kosher. Eva Hoffman describes how food was the means to rebel against religious norms (or to comply with them.) Her parents, after having survived the war, still complied with the dietary laws; they fasted on Yom Kippur and observed the dietary prohibitions of Passover. But Pani Ruta, who is the mother of Eva's friend, takes her to a restaurant during the fast of Yom Kippur, which is the holiest day for the Jews and "does the most shocking thing possible, ordering pork cutlets for herself and Eva" (Hoffman, 36). After their arrival in Canada, her little sister Alinka is sent to a Hebrew school "ironically, as a gesture of assimilation..." (144).

This shows how the times have changed in just a few decades, which have passed between Mary Antin's and Eva Hoffman's writing. Alinka, who grew up in postwar Eastern Europe, wants to make their household kosher upon her arrival in North America, but their mother "has no intention of going back to the kosher kitchen of her girlhood" (Hoffman, 144). Alinka belongs to the new generation of people, who return to their Jewish roots paradoxically as a way to assimilate in the New World, where ethnicity is gaining importance. Their mother belongs to previous generation, for whom the religion was a thing of the past.

Mona in Gish Jen's novel is a Chinese convert to Judaism (as the way to "be American.") She thinks a typical American problem is "people in America having... too many sources of calories already. For example, *latkes*" (301). Latkes are traditional fried pancakes made of potatoes, which are eaten on Chanukah, as a way to reminding the miracle of the oil in the Temple. For Mona it is a typical American food. She deep-fries them in a wok that Seth's stepmother gave her. This act is a symbolic mixing of cultures, or the "melting pot," this mixing of "wok" and "latkes," represents a mixture of Chinese and Jewish traditional foods, which curiously enough, can typically take place in America more than anywhere else. Mona's Jewish friend Seth eats everything – even the fat on her Auntie's red cooked pork, which is forbidden for Jews to eat. But Mona puts it aside. It is not clear whether her motives for not eating pork are conversion to Judaism, or are due to her belief this dish is too fattening – a typically American problem.

In Tova Reich's Mara, America is a kosher paradise. Reich mocks the religious establishment, which is materially thriving but spiritually starving. Mara's future husband and his mother came from Israel to the American land of plenty. A dinner is served in their honour.

> Thick steaks were served at dinner that night, and the juiciest slabs were placed before Sudah and his mother to demonstrate one of the matchless gifts of the United States. "You don't get stakes like that in Israel, now, do you?" Rose beamed. "Never mind, it's a young country" was Leon's comment... "You are right, Mrs. Lieb. In meat, who can compare? Also in other things America is best" "In what, for instance?" demanded Leon. Sudah waved the paper napkin that had been spread across his thighs. "In this. Also, toilet paper."
> Leon leaned over his plate and clenched a rabbinical fist. "You can live without meat for your mouth or paper for your *myeh,* but you can't live without food for your spirit." (Reich, 48-49)

Eating is not just alleviating hunger in the book. In both Judaism and Christianity Eve, who represents all women, has been blamed for eating forbidden fruit and seducing Adam. Mara rebels against male authority in her life by eating or rather "devouring" non-kosher chicken: "she considered, as she devoured the rubbery flesh, how with each bite she was defying two men, her kosher father and her vegetarian husband" (Reich, 177). It is an act of defiance against traditions which despise and exclude women.

Chicken seems to be a very important figure for American Jewish writers. In Shalom Auslander's short story "God is a Big Happy Chicken," the main character Yankel Morgenstern dies and goes to heaven, where it turns out that God is a large chicken. The name of the story evokes associations with American tendency to name everything "happy." Yankel is shocked, how can it be, what about the Bible? Archangel Gabriel who goes by the name "Gabe," tells him not to worry about the Bible, since "the joker who wrote that thing down" is in hell. Yankel longs to return to earth to tell his family that they can finally enjoy eating everything they want. "Oh, the years I wasted!...Nine children...Let them drive on Saturday, let them eat bacon, let them get the lunch special at Red Lobster!..They can watch television on Friday night...Not chosen. Just...people" (168-70). Gabe lets him return to Earth since "Chicken doesn't care." Morgenstern wants to tell his family about his discovery, but he sees the beauty of the Shabbos table and just cannot bring himself to reveal the truth to them. Auslander ridicules religion in general and the importance of food in the Jewish tradition in particular. At the same time the story concludes with the scene of a beautiful peaceful family meal, where the main character invents religion, which he has lost, because on earth people need it to survive.

Michael Chabon describes "strange days" in Yiddish Policemen's Union, a detective story set in an alternate version of the present day, where a temporary settlement for Yiddish-speaking Jewish refugees of the World War Two was established on Alaska. There are signs indicating the imminent coming of the Messiah. One of the miracles is happening at a kosher slaughterhouse "...a chicken turned on the shohet as he raised the ritual knife and announced, in Aramaic, the imminent advent of the Messiah." (13) The chicken also made predictions of future but still ended up being in a soup. The main protagonist thinks that strange times to be a Jew are also strange times to be a chicken. A chicken is so important in the Jewish culture, that it becomes a harbinger of the messiah.

Food has symbolic meaning in Dara Horn's novel The World to Come. An unborn character is in a world where all souls dwell before birth and after death. In this world, written word is consumed in the form of wine. The soon-to-be born Daniel meets Rosalie, who is a sommelier at his local paradise bar. After he tastes a bottle of Genesis he soon becomes a *biblioholic*. Rosalie brings him bottles of Exodus, Isaiah and Ezekiel from the cellar. She has a particular fondness of Hebrew and Yiddish vineyards. He sips poems from a bottle by Yiddish poets. In this imaginary world works of art are the nutrition of unborn souls.

A symbol of Israel connected to nourishment is used in Tova Reich's Master of the Return. When her child is returned, Ivriya Himmelhoch feeds her son with milk and honey. It is the symbol of the Land of Israel : "And I am come down to deliver them out of the hand of the Egyptians, and to bring them up out of that land unto a good land and a large, unto a land flowing with milk and honey" (Exodus 3:8, King James Bible). "Not for one second did she take her eyes off the child as he ate the bread and the honey and drank the milk. This was mother food...Flowing with milk and honey. For the sake of this milk and this honey, you must speak no ill of the land, and of its inhabitants say no unkind word" (Reich, 240). This is the final phrase in the novel, summing up the attitude to the Holy Land which is at the same time the mother figure. It refers to the biblical story from Numbers 13, which tells about the sin of the spies, who were sent to find out about the Land of Israel and returned speaking ill of it.

Tova Mirvis describes the history of kosher food in America in The Outside World. American manufacturers targeted the Jewish public and launched campaigns to attract Jewish customers.

> In the beginning, there was Crisco, an all-vegetable product, cheap and kosher, as its advertisements proclaimed in the Yiddish press. .. A few years later, Maxwell House, Quaker Oats and Post cereal became kosher and ran ads announcing this fact. In 1923, the OC, the first official national kosher certification, appeared on a can of Heinz vegetarian baked beans and a new world was born. In 1926, a dozen companies bore the OC imprint. By 1956, the OC was on a thousand products. Every historic highlight... the first kosher bottle of Coca-Cola...the first kosher frozen pizza, the first kosher Budweiser." (145-146)

The Coca-Cola, which is one of the symbols of popular American culture, bears the kosher sign. In this way, a significant part of American culinary culture becomes accessible to the observant population, which is living in a different world having built an insulated wall against assimilation. They "assimilate" American food to their needs; typical American food becomes kosher and in this way Jewish, too. The main character and her newly-wed husband are going to Memphis to open a kosher food store and restaurant. Her father says:

> We're going to have genuine Jewish food like your bubby made...Kasha varnishkes, potato knishes, matzo ball soup, kugel, homemade gefilte fish, chopped liver..I want the real thing...Gefilte fish can be the next sushi. You want to know why? Because people are hungry for something authentic. They remember when they used to eat it at their bubby and zaidy's house. They miss the past. Even if they never had it, they still miss it. (Mirvis, 152)

It seems food is the way of going back in time and space, to grandparents' house in a shtetl. It is grandmother's delicious Eastern European food beckoning from the past people long to return to.

In The Ladies Auxiliary, Tova Mirvis describes the religious rituals, cooking and preparations for holidays and recipes at great length. The novel is set in a small Orthodox community in Memphis, Tennessee.

It starts with a description of tornados which sweep across Arkansas every year. When it's over, people sigh with relief that "once again, we have been passed over" (Mirvis, 9). This is an allusion to Passover, when the Jewish homes were passed over by the tenth plague of Egypt.

Mirvis uses a first person plural "we" denoting the ladies of the community.

The development of the plot moves from holiday to holiday, thus making a

Jewish life circle an important part of the plot. The rituals are described in great detail, with explanations of their meaning. It familiarizes the reader with the rituals, letting an outsider to take a glimpse in the life of a closed Orthodox community. The complete story in the Scroll of Esther which is read on Purim is retold in short. The tradition of sending presents for Purim with cooking recipes is described in detail as well.

> We also busied ourselves with preparing our shaloch manot...The one thing we included...every year were hamentashen, the triangular cookies reminiscent of the three-cornered hat the evil Haman wore. But no two recipes were the same. The trick was in the filling. We used prune and poppyseed, apricot jelly and chocolate chips. (Mirvis, 244)

Each time of year is connected to a holiday:

> These next seven weeks were a bridge that linked the holidays of Pesach and Shavuot. On Pesach we left Egypt, and on Shavuot we received the Torah at Mount Sinai. The time in between transformed a group of slaves into a nation about to meet its God. In the time of the temple the omer offering was brought during these seven weeks. (Mirvis, 292)

She explains the rules connected to building a Tabernacle for the holiday of Sukkot, so that it is almost a "how-to" manual:

> We build our sukkahs out of all sorts of things: aluminium walls, canvas tarps, and metal poles, boards of plywood, old vinyl shower curtains. The sukkahs must have at least two and a half walls and the roofs must be made out of material that grows from the ground - small tree branches, clusters of leaves, or bamboo poles- spaced thinly enough that we can see the stars shining through at night but thick enough that there is more shade than sun during the day. (142-3)

Most of the characters in the novel are female. They are the decision-makers who hold in their hands the destiny and continuity of the community. Mirvis's figures are not feminist, but in their roles as mothers and wives they are the keepers of the people, upholders of the tradition. Theirs is the most important part. By keeping the holidays, making Jewish homes and preparing food they fulfill the important role of the traditional Jewish woman.

> At sundown, we lit Shabbos candles in our silver candelabras - one candle for each member of our families - and a calm settled over the neighborhood. Cars were parked, televisions were shut off, phones stopped ringing...We put on flowing skirts, silk blouses and fresh makeup. We were commanded to set the Sabbath apart and make it holy. We have clothing we wear only on Showbiz, china dishes, sterling silverware...We don't turn lights on and off, don't listen to music,go to work, use our ovens, our telephones, our cars. We reserve the day for

God and for family, spending those twenty-five hours between Friday's sundown and Saturday's dusk in a peaceful pattern of prayers, meals and relaxation. The outside world vanishes, even if only for that one day.

Alone in our houses, we waited for our husbands and children to come home from shul. We could have gone to shul if we wanted...we weren't obligated to go. That was only required of men; we could fulfill our religious obligations at home. (Mirvis, 18-19)

The detailed description proceeds to depict the Sabbath meal, which songs are sung and why, the blessing recited over a cup of wine, and over the challah bread. On Sabbath morning at the synagogue, the kiddush is recited, Mirvis gives the full quote in English translation: "Remember the Sabbath Day and keep it holy. For six days you may work, but the seventh day is the Sabbath, for Hashem your God" (Mirvis, 35). "Hashem" means "the Name" in Hebrew and is used by religious Jews instead of pronouncing God's name which is pronounced only in prayer, in order not to mention it in vain. This is a sign of piety, which the writer conveys for the initiated reader. The ceremony of end of Sabbath, the separation between Sabbath and the rest of the week is described as following:

...when three stars were visible, our husbands ended Shabbos with havdalah, praising God who separates between holy and secular, between light and darkness, between the seventh day of rest and six days of work. The braided candle shone before us, leading the way into this new week. We smelled the besamim, the cinnamon and cloves meant to console us as Shabbos was leaving, and we dipped the candle into the wine, watching the blue flames crackle and then go out. (Mirvis, 265)

Some words are not translated - *havdalah, besamim,* but their meaning can be derived from the context, which explains the ceremony.

Mirvis describes even such "secret" event as the immersion in a ritual bath, which is a commandment of a special importance for women. "The mikva was one of the pillars of Judaism, as important as observing Shabbos and keeping kosher..." (Mirvis, 64) We accompany the character through one of the most intimate moments of a Jewish woman's life. "Tziporah walked down the steps into the water. She dunked once and said the blessing: Blessed are you God, King of the universe who sanctifies us with His commandments and commands us to ritually immerse"(65).

Preparations for Passover are very important and include a huge cleaning endeavour:

> We finally finished cleaning, certain not a drop of chametz was in our possession, not between the pages of any books, not in our children's toys, our coat pockets, between our couch pillows, behind our beds, in our cars, our mailboxes, our garages, our bathrooms. Now it was time for cooking. We took out our Pesach dishes from the closets, attics, and cabinets where they had been stored since the year before. After we finished each recipe, there wasn't time to pause; we pulled out the ingredients for the next dish. We did what we could to get by without flour and other chametz; we made cakes with matza meal and potatoes in every possible form – fried, mashed, boiled, and stuffed. (284)

Mirvis's The Outside World ends with a beautiful scene of Passover Seder, where every details on a table is a symbol. "They told the story with words and with food..."(312). The continuity and of the Jewish tradition is presented through the symbolic meal, commemorating the Exodus from Egypt, which, the tradition says, should be remembered in every generation by every Jew. The story-telling is connected with eating of certain foods in a certain order.

According to Ezra Cappell, "the Passover seder is the ritualized ceremony of collective memory for the Jewish people. In the seder, communal liturgy and ritual are combined with a familial and culinary experience orchestrated to pass on the collective memory of Jewish history" (127).

> All over the world, seders were beginning and ending. Across time zones, there was a progression of wine drunk, parsley dipped, stories told. There were vegetarian seders and interfaith peace seders and feminist seders and liberation seders. Communal seders, seders overlooking the beach, seders next door to casinos, and traditional seders led by bearded grandfathers sitting at the heads of long tables...
>
> Karpas, the sprigs of parsley dipped into salt water. The green, a sign of spring. The salt, a memory of tears. Sadness and deliverance in the same bite...
>
> (Mirvis, Outside World, 307-310)

But there is an additional cup at the table – next to Elijah's cup there is a cup of Miriam, a female prophet. Just as eating "forbidden meat" is a symbol of forsaking Judaism, here the traditional meal of Passover seder symbolizes the ancient tradition, from the biblical Exodus and the long line of rabbis to modern-day America. But here, the cup of Miriam is a sign of change, signifying the importance of women's part, not only serving the meal, but also actively participating in it.

Passover seder has become one of the major tropes in American literary culture very early. Hana Wirth-Nesher suggests that its prominence in American Jewish fiction may stem from becoming entangled with the Christian world and the American Puritan rhetoric. The holiday of Passover is connected to the return to the promised Land of Israel. In Puritan ideology, it is America, which becomes the New Jerusalem and the Jews of America have been required to renounce their claims for Israel as the promised land. (Liturgy, 118)

Passover serves as a reminder of lost Judaism and sometimes is a life-changing experience. Anne Roiphe describes in her memoir how she is invited to a Passover seder with her daughters by her religious doctor, after having written an article about having a Christmas tree and assimilation. "This, I understand, is his comment on my Christmas tree" (139). At the table, her daughter experiences a Seder for the first time in her life.

Anne Roiphe is afraid that only the male children will be allowed to ask the traditional four questions like it was when she was a child, but the girls read the questions now. The story of the exodus and liberation from slavery is told in "incomprehensible Hebrew" and she is mesmerized by the sound of it and by the weight of the story (144). Roiphe feels re-connected to her religious experience through a ritual which is reenacted every year for thousands of years everywhere in the world where there are Jewish people. But is it coincidental, that she uses a male pronoun here?

> The Seder seems like a long pledge of allegiance in which each person at the table joins in reading and in the prayers and in so doing commits, connects himself to the flood tides of Jewish history, binds himself again to the tribe... The wine, the music, the rhythms of the repeated prayers, they are a kind of hocus-pocus clouding my reason, my good sense, my independence, my universality. Despite myself the distances close." (147)

The food, the language and the story are intertwined. The importance of the tradition is closely connected to a ritual having to do with food. Several weeks after the holiday, her daughter receives a book on the Holocaust. She reads it, then goes to the library and gets more and more books on the topic. Because she had accepted an invitation to the Seder, her daughter Katie has a different childhood than she might have had otherwise (147).

98

For the early immigrants who started eating non-kosher food, it served as the way to assimilate into American non-Jewish world, and today eating kosher food is the first step to return to Judaism.

Evidently, the themes connected to food are as relevant as ever and are used in many works of American Jewish fiction in different forms and contexts. Rituals connected with food connect Jewish characters to Judaism and show how the Jewish perspective on food and food making predominates every generation of Jews.

7. Conclusion

Literature cannot exist in a vacuum, and often it plays the role of a mirror of what is happening in the society. In the case of Jewish American writers, it is no exception. The diversity of thematic fields which are present in Jewish American literature shows how difficult it is or perhaps impossible to separate Judaism as a religion from Jewishness as a culture, as a way of life, and a system of social values. Just as many Americans are moving towards recapturing their multiple heritages, so the Jewish Americans are rediscovering the spiritual and religious dimensions of the Jewish tradition. How to define this tradition – whether in a broad sense, including cultural and linguistic aspects, or in a narrow sense of only ritual part, is a different matter.

Ritual is only one of many facets of Judaism, and it would be wrong to exclude other facets, which make the whole picture all the more fascinating. Judaism means much more than a set of rituals and cannot be separated from a general cultural tradition, a tradition which is now a part of general American culture. American culture undergoes a constant change and makes freedom of choice – even a choice of one's identity, one of the main pillars of its existence.

Everything which deals with the Jewish culture implies dealing with the topic of religion – whether denying or embracing it. Maybe it is too far-fetched to argue that everything that exists in American Jewish literature is a new American Talmud. But there is no doubt that most of the writers, no matter whether they are secular or observant, deal with the Jewish religious culture at one or the other angle.

In America, a country which sees it itself as the bearer of Judeo-Christian civilization, the moral codes and values of Christianity and Judaism are interconnected. The idea of equality for everyone, no matter what creed or class, fascinated thinkers and made America a symbol of freedom for many nations of the world. Thus, America aspires to be "a light unto the nations," the idea being similar to the Jewish idea of a chosen people, chosen to be a moral example to other nations of the world. In Nathan Englander's story "The Wig," an elderly Orthodox wigmaker summarizes the opinion that is important in an attempt to understand the role America played in Jewish collective consciousness:"That is the wonder of this country. Jews have rights; women have rights" (98). America has become a haven for Jews, who fled the persecution and pogroms of Europe. In the Jewish tradition, there is no "competition" with the promised Land of Israel which was promised by God to Abraham and his descendants in the covenant. But for American Jews, the loyalty to a promised land is a controversial issue, since there was hardly any country in history which gave more freedom and where the religious affiliation played smaller role in achieving the "American dream" of freedom and happiness.

Anne Roiphe expresses the feelings of many of her "between the worlds" generation, when she says that in the end the promise of Americanization made to her father, "has gone sour." "I don't feel a real part of this nation because at bottom I am a Jew. After Germany only in Israel can a Jew feel really connected and I am not enough of a Jew to go to Israel" (212). The Promised Land, as a place where one is at least not persecuted for religious beliefs was enough for the first generation immigrants. But their grandchildren are not satisfied. They are seeking milk and honey in the Promised Land of their forefathers, going back to the false promised lands where their grandparents fled from, and seeking to find out what was promised and to whom in the first place.

Whether the Jewish American writers are writing within or outside of the Jewish tradition, it influences their writing in various ways: whether it is location – like Israel or other important places in the Jewish history, using Hebrew or Yiddish, or dealing with issues of Anti-Semitism or the Holocaust, or adopting folklore themes like Golem or Bible exegesis – they constantly tap into the Jewish sources. Most of the modern writers are secular people who nevertheless are connected to the tradition by various ways, which shows time and again how Judaism as a religion is inseparable from either their personal identities of from their literary journeys.

In 1976 Karl Shapiro wrote: "The problem of writer as Jew has shifted to Israel; in the United States at least it is a vestige. The hyphenated Jewish writer still exists in places where Jewish persecution is politically and religiously alive: in Russia and in the Arab nations, for instance"(6). The newest works of fiction show that "the problem of writer as Jew" does not exist indeed: it ceased to be a problem. The issues and themes did not lose their poignancy and relevance with the fourth generation of immigrants, quite on the contrary, they are interested to find out what their grandparents had left behind. If the early immigrant writers travelled from the Old World through the Ellis Island, many modern writers travelled backwards in time and space, often finding themselves outside of their native land of America. The importance of remembering cannot be underestimated in Judaism, most of the rituals are commemoration of events which took place thousands of years ago, like crossing the Red Sea or deliverance from slavery. As the common joke goes: "they tried to kill us, we won, now let's eat."

In this sense, the intertextuality of the contemporary Jewish literature in America is a way to perpetrate the Jewish tradition by interacting and reenacting traditional texts or legends. When writers go back to the countries they came from, they are writing a history of their people.

Mary Antin wanted to show how she was transformed from an Yiddish speaking immigrant to an "English-writing and-thinking-without-an accent" assimilated American. America liberates her from being "handicapped" by her femaleness and her Jewishness.

When Antin or Cahan's Levinsky describe their life in the Pale, one of their goals is to make the Jewish life accessible and understandable for a general non-Jewish American reader – therefore they create glossaries and explanations. Their fiction was the first step in bridging the gap between "insider" writing and mainstream discourse, but their understanding of the Jewish tradition was superficial and limited to a description of rituals without deep spiritual meaning. It corresponded to the situation in their era, when Orthodox Judaism was considered too ritualistic, inconvenient and relevant only for the Old World.

Andrew Furman notes that in the post-immigrant generation of the 1950's and 60's, Jewish authors reached the mainstream audience by creating protagonists with whom the mainstream reading public could identify. "While these characters, like their authors, were nominally Jewish and carried with them certain unmistakable ethnic markers (their yiddishisms, their semitic features, etc.) their more salient qualities of alienation and marginality were qualities with which non-Jews could readily identify" ("The Jewishness of the Contemporary Gentile Writer", 5). These protagonists were "anything but parochial," they were out in the outside world, establishing their place in it.

Stanley Chyet suggests that Roth, Bellow and Malamud "testify to demoralization of Anglo-Saxon nativism in America" (41).

Their characters struggle with universal human issues, exploring the personalities, not "exploiting them as vehicles for doctrines or creeds of any sort" (37). Contemporary writers often go even further and transform their characters to newly Orthodox, identity-seeking, returning-to-the roots Jewish individuals, who find Judaism, which empowers and gives them meaning.

The theme of return is a common motive in contemporary Jewish American writing. The name of the novel Master of the Return by Tova Reich is a direct translation of a Hebrew expression *"Baal tshuva"* which literally means "Master of Return" and translates as a Jewish person returning to religion.

Mark Krupnik explains: "If the writers of the 1930s and 1940s were bent on escape, the most recent generation has been committed to a return" (qtd in Meyer, 110-111).

An important part of today's writing are the women writers, who reclaim the traditionally male Jewish tradition and create female characters who are self-confident, intellectual, educated and knowledgeable both in secular and in Jewish issues. These characters open a whole new world of Jewish feminist discourse, which stands in contrast to early immigrant writers, for whom Judaism was connected to backward patriarchal world they were only glad to have left behind.

The question which side of the hyphen is more important – the Jewish or the American, has not lost its relevance in a few generations which have passed since the first immigrants reached the shores of their new homeland.

Antin's prophetic words: "My grandchildren, for all I know, may have a graver task than I have set them. Perhaps they may have to testify that the faith of Israel is a heritage that no heir in the direct line has the power to alienate from his successors... What positive affirmation of the persistence of Judaism in the blood my descendants may have to make, I may not be present to hear" (195), have come to fulfilment in the fiction of Tova Mirvis, where rituals and customs are described with deep knowledge and understanding in a positive light.

In the immigrant novels, the act of entering mainstream American literature meant distancing oneself from the Jewish topics, trying to bridge the differences between Americans and immigrants by explaining their "strange ways" and trying to close the gap by adjusting to the "American ways" of the white Christian majority. The path that went from assimilation to universalist humanistic values made a full circle and turned back to pre-American and even pre-European roots which acquired a new meaning and understanding.

A. Furman points out that Cynthia Ozick anticipated in her series of early essays published in the 70's a new wave of Jewish writers who created "post-assimilated protagonists – observant Jews often living in insular Orthodox communities -- overtly grappling with issues of Jewish history and theology." Ozick's vision was supplanting a mere ethnic fiction with Judaic, or "liturgical" fiction ("The Jewishness", 6). Furman calls this development "a literary revolution," invoking the Judaic concept of *tshuva* or return to religion, a phenomenon which is described by many critics as a Jewish literary movement of return. He regrets the tendency of contemporary Jewish novelists to look increasingly inward for their inspiration, while their protagonists increasingly retreat from the larger, secular society (7).

I disagree with the point of view, that this trend makes the Jewish American writers less universal or less interesting for the broader cultural conversation. I believe they bring the internal Jewish discourse into the mainstream American cultural discourse, and make it available for the general non-Jewish American audience by dealing with and explaining Jewish cultural and religious topics. These writers expect their audiences to accept them as they are, they are not apologizing for being less universal by throwing away their heritage.

Taking it further, some writers like Tova Mirvis create a sort of a "textbook" on Judaism, where the reader gets explanations of a traditional worldview of Judaism, as well as many rituals and holidays. It wakes positive interest in the Jewish tradition and serves to widen the Jewish literacy of the general American audience. Jewish literacy is becoming a common knowledge and a part of a mainstream American culture, where Jewish rituals like Chanukah are not alien anymore and are celebrated in public or Jewish weddings and funerals are shown in popular movies.

Jewish culture has changed under influence of American culture, which in turn changed and embraced the cultures of immigrants, which became a part of general American mainstream culture. A. Furman thinks that works by Gentile writers who create Jewish protagonists might signify a new trend toward the Jewishness of an increasing number of non-Jewish writers. He suggests that their work should be included in curriculum of Jewish American fiction, just as Human Stain should be read in courses on African American literature. (The Jewishness, 15-16). Perhaps this suggestion is the only way to deal with the complicated world of shifting identities which can be discarded and re-acclaimed.

As Ezra Cappell points out: " In present-day America, Orthodoxy, the words of the Torah, the laws of *Halachah,* Jewish ritual praxis, are no longer exotic. This trend is powerfully reflected in the fiction that has been produced in the past thirty years in America, a fascinating development that has only gained momentum in the new millennium" (173). This mutual influence is what makes American culture diverse and interesting.

Various ethnic and immigrant literatures have had a great success in the mainstream American reader. In an essay written in 1972, Stanley Chyet quotes Meyer Levin, who wrote as late as 1950, that "a book about Jews" would "never be regarded as in the direct mainstream of American writing" (31).

It only shows how fast notions of mainstream American writing can change, and how quickly immigrant cultures have become a part of general American culture. It is beyond doubt that the Jewish religious and cultural tradition has found its secure place in Jewish American writing. And the Jewish American writing has become a part of American culture.

8. Works cited:

Adler, Rachel. „The Jew Who Wasn't There." On Being a Jewish Feminist.
Ed. S. Heschel. New York: Schocken, 1983. 3-12.

Anolik, Ruth Bienstock. "Reviving the Golem: Cultural Negotiations in
Ozick's The Puttermesser Papes and Piercy's He She and It." Studies in
American Jewish Literature. 19 (2000): 37-48.

Antin, Mary. The Promised Land. 1912. New York: Penguin Books, 1997.

Auslander, Shalom. Beware of God. 2005. London: Picador, 2006.

Biale, David. Eros and the Jews. From Biblical Israel to Contemporary
America. Berkeley: University of California Press, 1997.

Biale, Rachel. Women and Jewish Law. An Exploration of Women's Issues in
Halakhic Sources. New York: Schocken Books, 1984.

Bible: New Standard American Bible.
<http://bible.cc/jeremiah/31-15.htm≥20 Jan. 2009
King James Bible <http://bible.cc/exodus/3-8.htm> 20 Jan. 2009.

Bumble, Anna Petrov. "Intellectual Jewish Woman vs. the JAP in the Works of
American Jewish Women Writers." Studies in American Jewish Literature.
19 (2000): 26-36.

Cahan, Abraham. The Rise of David Levinsky. 1917. New York: Penguin:
1993.

Cappell, Ezra. American Talmud. The Cultural Work of Jewish American
Fiction. Albany: SUNY Press, 2007.

Chabon, Michael. 2007. The Yiddish Policemen's Union. New York: Harper,
2008.

Chyet, Stanley F. "Three Generations: An Account of American Jewish Fiction
(1896 – 1969)." Jewish Social Studies 34.1 (1972) : 31-41.

Cohen, Rose. Out of the Shadow. A Russian Jewish Girlhood on the Lower
East Side. 1918. Ithaca: Cornell UP, 1995.

Cooper, John. Eat and Be Satisfied. A Social History of Jewish Food.
Northvale, New Jersey: Jason Aronson Inc., 1993.

Diner, Hasja. A New Promised Land. A History of Jews in America. Oxford
UP, 2000.

---. Hungering for America. Italian, Irish, and Jewish Foodways in the Age of Migration. Harvard UP, 2001.

---. Lower East Side Memories, a Jewish place in America. Princeton and Oxford: Princeton UP, 2000.

---. The Jews of the United States, 1654 to 2000. London: University of California Press, 2004.

Englander, Nathan. For the Relief of Unbearable Urges. 1999. New York: Vintage, 2000.

Fellman, Jack. The Revival of a Classical Tongue. Eliezer Ben Yehuda and the Modern Hebrew Language. The Hague: Mouton, 1973.

Fischer, Pascal "Voices of Identity. Language in Jewish-American Literature." Anglophone Jewish Literature. Ed. Alex Staehler. London: Routledge, 2000. 211-224.

Foer, Jonathan Safran. 2002. Everything is Illuminated. London: Penguin, 2003.

Furman, Andrew. Israel through the Jewish American Imagination. A Survey of Jewish American Literature in Israel. 1928-1995. Albany: SUNY Press, 1997.

---. "Immigrant Dreams and Civic Promises: (Con-) Testing Identity in Early Jewish American Literature and Gish Jen's Mona in the Promised Land." Melus, 25.1. (2000): 209-226.

---. "The Jewishness of the Contemporary Gentile Writer: Zadie Smith's The Autograph Man." Melus 30.1, (2005): 3-17.

Haggard-Gilson, Nancy. "The Construction of Jewish American Identity in Novels of the Second Generation." Studies in American Jewish Literature 11.1 (1992): 22-35.

Harshav, Benjamin. Language in Time of Revolution. Berkeley: University of California Press, 1993.

---. The Meaning of Yiddish. Berkeley: University of California Press, 1990.

Harap, Louis. „The Religious Art of Cynthia Ozick." Judaism 33.4 (1984): 353-363.

Hoffman, Eva. 1989. Lost in Translation. A Life in a New Language. London:Vintage, 1998.

Horn, Dora. In the Image 2002. New York: Norton, 2003.

---. The World to Come. New York: Norton, 2006.

Goldstein, Rebecca. Mazel. New York: Viking, 1995.

---. Mind-Body Problem. 1983. New York: Penguin, 1993.

Gottstein-Strobl, Christine. The "Pursuit of Jewishness." Jüdisch-
    Amerikanische Literatur der Gegenwart. Frankfurt am Main: IKO –
    Verlag für Interkulturelle Kommunikation, 2007.

James, Henry. The American Scene. 1907. London: Granville Publishing,
    1987.

Jen, Gish. Mona in the Promised Land. 1997. London: Granta Books, 1998.

Jong, Erica. "How I Got to Be Jewish." Who We Are. On Being (and Not
Being) a Jewish American Writer. Ed. Derek Rubin. New York: Schocken,
2005. 99-113.

Kalinsky, Jenna. "Great, My Daughter is Marrying a Nazi." The Modern
Jewish Girl's Guide to Guilt. Ed. Ruth Andrew Ellenson, 2005. New York:
Plume, 2006. 231-244.

Kauvar, Elaine M. "Cynthia Ozick's Book of Creation: "Puttermesser and
    Xantippe." Contemporary Literature 26.1 (1985): 40-54.

Kirschenbaum, Blossom S. "Tova Reich's Fiction: Perspectives on Mothering."
    Connections and Collisions. Identities in Contemporary Jewish-
American Women's Writing. Ed. Lois R. Rubin. Newark: University of
Delaware Press, 2005. 71-109.

Klingenstein, Susanne. "In Life I am not Free." The Writer Cynthia Ozick and
    Her Jewish Obligations." Daughters of Valor: Contemporary Jewish
    American Women Writers. Eds. Jay L. Halio and Ben Siegel. Newark:
    University of Delaware Press, 1997. 48-80.

...., "Visits to Germany in Modern American Jewish Writing." Contemporary
    Literature 34.3 (1993): 538-570.

Lewin, Judith. "Diving into the Wreck": Binding Oneself to Judaism
    Contemporary Jewish Women's Fiction." Shofar 26. 3 (2008): 48-67.

Meyer, Adam. "Putting the "Jewish" back in "Jewish American Fiction": a Look
at Jewish American Fiction from 1977 to 2002 and an Allegorical Reading
of Nathan Englander's "The Gilgul of Park Avenue." Shofar 22. 3 (2004):
104-120.

Mirvis, Tova. The Outside World 2004. Piatkus: London, 2005.

---. The Ladies Auxiliary 1999. Ballantine: New York, 2000.

Oster, Judith. Crossing Cultures. Creating Identity in Chinese and Jewish
    American Literature. Columbia: University of Missouri Press, 2003.

Ozick, Cynthia. The Puttermesser Papers. New York: Knopf, 1997.

Piercy, Marge. He, She and It. New York: Fawsett Books, 1991.

---. Sleeping with Cats. 2002. New York: Perennial-Harper, 2003.

Reich, Tova. Mara. 1978. Syracuse, N.Y: Syracuse UP, 2001.

---. Master of the Return. 1988. Syracuse, N.Y: Syracuse UP, 1999.

---. The Jewish War. 1995. Syracuse, N.Y: Syracuse UP, 1997.

Rischin, Moses. 1962. The Promised City. New York's Jews 1870- 1914.
    Cambridge, London: Harvard UP, 1977.

Roiphe, Anne. Generation Without Memory. New York: The Linden Press.
    Simon, 1987.

Ronell, Anne P. "Rebecca Goldstein: Tension and Ambivalence." Modern
Jewish Women Writers in America. Ed. Evelyn Avery. Palgrave Macmillian,
    2007. 151- 173.

Roth, Philip. Letting Go. 1961. New York: Farrar,1982.

---. The Counterlife. New York: Farrar, 1986.

Satlof, Claire R. "History, Fiction and the Tradition: Creating a Jewish
    Feminist Poetic."On Being a Jewish Feminist. Ed. S. Heschel. New
    York: Schocken, 1983. 186-207.

Seidman, Naomi. Marriage Made in Heaven. The Sexual Politics of Hebrew
    and Yiddish. Berkeley: University of California Press, 1997.

Shapiro, Karl. "The American-Jewish Writer." Melus 3.2, The Contemporary
    Writer and His Sense of Ethnicity. (1976): 6-9.

Shandler, Jeffrey. Adventures in Yiddishland: Postvernacular Language &
    Culture. Berkeley: University of California Press, 2005.

Shapiro, Lauri Gwen. "Oy Christmas Tree, Oy Christmas Tree." The Modern
    Jewish Girl's Guide to Guilt. Ed. Ruth Andrew Ellenson, 2005. New
    York: Plume, 2006. 219-230.

Sivan, Miriam. "Cynthia Ozick's Puttermesser and Bleilip: Dualism and
    Redemption. " American@ Vol. I, Issue. 2, 89-101. 05 May 2006.
    <http://www.uhu.es/hum676/revista/sivan.pdf >

109

Sollors, Werner. Introduction. The Promised Land. By Mary Antin. New York: Penguin, 1997. XI-L.

Stahlberg, Lesleigh Cushing. "The Opposite of Jewish: On Remembering and Keeping in Contemporary Jewish American Fiction." Shofar 25.3 (2007): 72-90.

Uffen, Ellen Serlen. Strands of the Cable : the Place of the Past in Jewish American Women's Writing. New York : Lang, 1992.

Wirth-Nesher, Hana. "Accented Imagination." Imagining the American Jewish Community. Ed. Jack Werthheimer. Waltham: Brandeis UP, 2007. 286-303.

---. Call it English. The Languages of Jewish American Literature. Princeton: Princeton UP, 2006.

---. "Magnified and Sanctified: Liturgy in Recent Jewish American Literature." Ideology and Jewish Identity in Israeli and American Literature. Ed. Emily Miller Budick. Albany: State U of New York P, 2001. 115-30.

---. "Traces of the past: multilingual Jewish American writing." The Cambridge Companion to Jewish American Literature. Ed. Michael P. Kramer, Hana Wirth-Nesher. Cambridge UP, 2003. 100-128.

Umansky, Ellen M. "Jewish Women in the 20th-Century U.S." Jewish Women in Historical Perspective. Ed. Judith R. Baskin. Detroit: Wayne State University Press, 1991. 265-286.

Yezierska, Anzja. The Breadgivers. 1925. New York: Persea Books, 2003.

Zacharasiewicz, Waldemar. Images of Germany in American Literature. Iowa City: University of Iowa Press, 2007.

Zucker, David J. "Midrash and Modern American Literature." Studies in American Jewish Literature 11.1 (1992): 7-21.

<http://www.hebrewsongs.com/song-kolhaolamkulo.htm > 05.01.2009

<http://www.ushmm.org/museum/mission/ > 21.01.2009

9. Abstract (Zusammenfassung)

In der Magisterarbeit handelt es sich um die Rolle der Religion in der modernen
jüdisch-amerikanischen Literatur. Die Suche nach den Wurzeln ist ein Trend in
der amerikanischen Gesellschaft geworden. Dieser Trend widerspiegelt sich
auch in Kunst und Literatur.

Die Gesellschaft wandelt sich von einem "Schmelztiegel" in eine
multiethnische und multikulturelle Gesellschaft. Viele Autoren wenden sich in
ihren Werken an die Kultur ihrer Vorfahren. Die jüdisch-amerikanische
Literatur ist auch ein Beispiel hierfür. Es ist fast unmöglich, die Kultur von der
Religion zu trennen, denn wenn es sich um jüdische Themen handelt, geht es
um die Kultur, die eng mit der jüdischen Religion verbunden ist.

Judentum ist eine Religion, die mit Zeit und Geschichte eng verbunden ist.
Selbst wenn Autoren sich mit säkularen Themen beschäftigen, gibt es trotzdem
eine Anbindung an die religiöse Problematik. Viele moderne Werke sind von
Autoren geschrieben, die fundiertes Wissen vom Judentum haben, sie benutzen
oft jüdische Sprachen, Figuren aus der Folklore und religiöse Ideen.

Es gibt einen großen Unterschied zwischen den frühen Werken von
Immigranten und den modernen Werken der amerikanisch-jüdischen Autoren
der dritten Generation. Während die Immigrantenautoren sich bemüht haben,
sich so schnell wie möglich zu assimilieren und die Welt der Väter hinter sich
zu lassen, haben die jüngsten Autoren in ihren Werken die jüdischen Themen
neu entdeckt.

Für die Autoren der ersten Generation war das Erlernen der englischen Sprache
sehr wichtig.

Die Autoren von heute haben Englisch als Muttersprache. Sie schreiben
zwar auf Englisch, benutzen aber sehr häufig Begriffe oder Ausdrücke, die
nicht erklärt oder übersetzt sind aus den jüdischen Sprachen Hebräisch und
Jiddisch. Jüdische Literatur war immer multilingual.

Hebräisch ist die Sprache der Liturgie und Jiddisch ist die Sprache des
Europäischen Judentums. Nach dem Holocaust wurden die meisten Sprecher
des Jiddischen ausgerottet. Das ist der Grund, warum Jiddisch heute eine Rolle
der "heiligen Sprache" spielt und in dieser Hinsicht an die Stelle des

Hebräischen rückt. Das moderne Hebräisch ist die Staatssprache Israels und hat
die Position der Alltagssprache genommen.

Viele Schriftsteller benutzen jüdische Namen, die nicht übersetzt werden
und die wichtige Bedeutung für die Entwicklung der Figur haben.
Die Autoren setzen bei den Lesern gute Kenntnisse von religiöser Thematik
voraus. Das sind zum Beispiel Abschnitte aus der Liturgie oder aus den
religiösen Quellen wie die Bibel oder Talmud.

Der Themenkreis hat oft eine Verbindung mit Judentum, zum Beispiel
wenn es um bestimmte Figuren geht wie Golem, eine Figur, die man aus der
Folklore kennt. Die jüdische Thematik wird in das neue, positive Licht gestellt.
Viele Romane benutzen jüdische Settings in Amerika, wie Lower East Side,
oder Israel, oder europäische Länder, aus denen Juden nach Amerika
ausgewandert sind.

Israel ist ein sehr wichtiger Ort für die jüdische Weltauffassung. Er ist eng
verbunden mit dem Glauben. Die Werke von vielen Autoren benutzen Israel als
Hintergrund. Seit der Entstehung des jüdischen Staates wurde Israel zum
Zentrum der jüdischen Identität für viele Juden überall auf der Welt. Für
amerikanische Juden, die in Amerika ihr gelobtes Land fanden, spielt Israel
eine konkurrierende Rolle. Manchmal müssen die Figuren zwischen jüdischer
und amerikanischer Loyalität entscheiden.

Auch Europa, zum Beispiel Ukraine und Deutschland sind oft als Settings
benutzt. Oft kehren die Figuren im Roman zurück nach Europa, um nach ihren
Wurzeln zu suchen. Das entspricht dem allgemeinen Trend in der Gesellschaft.
Das ist das Gegenteil von den frühen Immigrantengeschichten, in denen die
Bewegung aus Europa nach Amerika, die oft als neue Geburt gesehen war,
dargestellt wurde.

Ein wichtiger Teil der heutigen Entwicklung ist die Suche nach
Möglichkeit, Judentum und Feminismus zu vereinbaren. Viele Autoren
verarbeiten die traditionelle männliche Tradition und suchen nach Bedeutung
der Religion als Frauen. Im traditionellen Judentum war die Rolle der Frau auf
die Haushaltsangelegenheiten begrenzt. Frauen durften heilige Texte nicht
studieren. Die Rolle der jüdischen Frau war, Mutter und Frau von einem
Gelehrten zu sein. Diese Situation war für viele Frauen unerträglich und hat

dazu geführt, dass sie der Religion den Rücken kehrten. Sie konnten sich als Frauen spirituell nicht entwickeln.

In der zweiten Hälfte des zwanzigsten Jahrhunderts beginnt eine religiöse Renaissance und viele Frauen entdecken Judentum für sich neu – als aktive Mitglieder der Gemeinde. Dieser Trend wird auch in der Literatur reflektiert. Manchmal haben männliche Autoren negative Stereotypen benutzt, zum Beispiel von der "jüdisch-amerikanischen Prinzessin." Viele Frauen haben das Gefühl, dass diese Stereotypen nicht richtig sind und wollen mit ihren Figuren intellektuelle selbstbewusste Frauen schaffen, für die auch die jüdische Tradition wichtig ist. In Werken von Mary Antin und A. Yezierska wird die jüdische Tradition als zurückgebliebener und patriarchalischer Überrest aus der alten Welt gesehen. In Amerika hat man als Frau viele Möglichkeiten, sich zu entwickeln. Die Religion gehört der Vergangenheit an, die so schnell wie möglich vergessen sein soll. Die modernen Autorinnen suchen mit ihren Figuren jüdische Spiritualität, sie sind oft kritisch der Religion gegenüber, möchten aber als Frauen die jüdische Tradition für sich neu entdecken.

Auch Essen ist ein wichtiges kulturelles Merkmal und wird in vielen Werken symbolisch benutzt und ausgearbeitet. Im jüdischen Glauben sind die Speisegesetze eines der wichtigsten Bestandteile des Lebens, sie dienen als ein "Identitätsmerkmal". Es gibt auch eine allgemeine Verbindung zwischen Essen und dem kollektiven Gedächtnis einer ethnischen oder religiösen Gruppe.

Mit der Rückkehr zur Religion ist diese Frage wichtiger als je. Viele Figuren kehren zur Religion zurück und fangen als erstes an, koscher zu essen. Das symbolisiert oft den Konflikt der Generationen, die "umgekehrte Assimilation."

Viele Autoren benutzen auch Symbole der wichtigen jüdischen Feiertage, wie Passah Fest oder Sabbat Essen.

So viele Themen sind mit der Religion verbunden, dass man keine klare Trennlinie zwischen der Religion und Kultur machen kann. Die Religion ist ein Teil der Kultur und Kultur ein Teil der Identität. Die Suche nach Identität ist ein wichtiger Trend in der heutigen Amerikanischen Gesellschaft, wo man nach kulturellen und ethnischen Wurzeln sucht. Jüdische Amerikaner entdecken ihre Kultur in allen Dimensionen, auch spirituellen und religiösen.

Es wäre aber nicht richtig, Judentum nur als Religion zu definieren. Alles, was mit jüdischer Thematik zu tun hat, hat auch mit Judentum zu tun. Amerika ist ein Land, dass allen ihren Bürgern Freiheit und Gleichheit verspricht, egal welcher Herkunft sie sind. Das macht Amerika außergewöhnlich in der jüdischen Geschichte, die voll von blutigen Verfolgungen ist. Amerika symbolisiert in den Augen der jüdischen Amerikaner "das gelobte Land."

Viele Enkelkinder von Immigranten suchen heute nach ihrer Identität, die ihre Großeltern zurückgelassen haben. Sie finden sie oft in ihren Wurzeln, die außerhalb Amerikas liegen.

Die Autoren, die am Anfang des zwanzigsten Jahrhunderts schrieben, mussten sich von ihrer Herkunft trennen, um in die "mainstream" Literatur zu gelangen. Heute ist amerikanisch-jüdische Literatur ein fester Teil von der allgemeinen amerikanischen Kultur. Die Autoren stellen nicht nur ethnische Juden dar, die über das Judentum nichts wissen, sondern Figuren, die nach Spiritualität und Bedeutung in ihrer Religion suchen. Das dient nicht der Ausgrenzung, sondern öffnet dem Leser die Möglichkeit, mehr über unterschiedlichen Kulturen und Traditionen zu erfahren.

Die jüdische religiöse und kulturelle Tradition hat ihren festen Platz in der amerikanischen Literatur und Kultur gefunden. Wie man die Tradition definiert, ob nur als rituelle Bräuche oder im weiteren kulturellen Sinn, bleibt offen.

Das Judentum ist aber viel mehr als nur eine Sammlung der Rituale und kann deswegen nicht von der Kultur getrennt werden, einer Kultur, die nun ein Bestandteil der allgemeinen amerikanischen Kultur ist.